Connect

SECOND EDITION

Jack C. Richards
Carlos Barbisan

with Chuck Sandy

Student's Book 4

Shaftesbury Road, Cambridge CB2 8EA, United Kingdom

One Liberty Plaza, 20th Floor, New York, NY 10006, USA

477 Williamstown Road, Port Melbourne, VIC 3207, Australia

314–321, 3rd Floor, Plot 3, Splendor Forum, Jasola District Centre, New Delhi – 110025, India

103 Penang Road, #05–06/07, Visioncrest Commercial, Singapore 238467

Cambridge University Press & Assessment is a department of the University of Cambridge.

We share the University's mission to contribute to society through the pursuit of education, learning and research at the highest international levels of excellence.

www.cambridge.org
Information on this title: www.cambridge.org/9781009683722

© Cambridge University Press & Assessment 2009

This publication is in copyright. Subject to statutory exception and to the provisions of relevant collective licensing agreements, no reproduction of any part may take place without the written permission of Cambridge University Press & Assessment.

First published 2004
Second Edition 2009

20 19 18 17 16 15 14 13 12 11 10 9 8 7 6 5 4 3 2 1

Printed in Great Britain by CPI Group (UK) Ltd, Croydon CR0 4YY

A catalogue record for this publication is available from the British Library

Library of Congress Cataloging-in-Publication Data
Richards, Jack C.
Connect / Jack C. Richards, Carlos Barbisan, with Chuck Sandy. – 2nd ed.
    p.   cm.
Summary: "Connect is a four-level, four-skills American English course for young adolescents. Connect encourages students to connect to English through contemporary, high-interest topics and contexts, fun dialogs, and games. Each student's book includes grammar and vocabulary presentations and a multi-skills, graded syllabus" – Provided by publisher.
ISBN 978-0-521-73721-0 (Student's bk. 4)
1. English language – Textbooks for foreign speakers. I. Barbisan, Carlos.
II. Sandy, Chuck. III. Title.
PE1128.R4553   2009
428.2'4–dc22

                              2008037556

ISBN   978-1-009-68372-2   Student's Book 4
ISBN   978-0-521-73725-8   Workbook 4
ISBN   978-0-521-73727-2   Teacher's Edition 4

Cambridge University Press & Assessment has no responsibility for the persistence or accuracy of URLs for external or third-party internet websites referred to in this publication and does not guarantee that any content on such websites is, or will remain, accurate or appropriate.

Art direction, book design, photo research, and layout services: Adventure House, NYC
Audio production: Full House, NYC

Table of Contents

Syllabus iv

Unit 1 My life
Lesson 1 Last summer 2
Lesson 2 A new school year 4
Mini-review 6
Lesson 3 Life events 8
Lesson 4 Then and now 10
Get Connected 12
Review 14

Unit 2 The Future
Lesson 5 Predictions 16
Lesson 6 When I'm older 18
Mini-review 20
Lesson 7 Teen Center 22
Lesson 8 After high school 24
Get Connected 26
Review 28

Unit 3 Plans
Lesson 9 Weekend plans 30
Lesson 10 Evening plans 32
Mini-review 34
Lesson 11 Making plans 36
Lesson 12 Vacation plans 38
Get Connected 40
Review 42

Unit 4 People
Lesson 13 Teens online 44
Lesson 14 Personality types 46
Mini-review 48
Lesson 15 Unusual people 50
Lesson 16 Who's that girl? 52
Get Connected 54
Review 56

Unit 5 Entertainment
Lesson 17 For fun 58
Lesson 18 Young entertainers 60
Mini-review 62
Lesson 19 Are you a fan? 64
Lesson 20 Pop culture trivia 66
Get Connected 68
Review 70

Unit 6 Experiences
Lesson 21 Taking risks 72
Lesson 22 What we've done 74
Mini-review 76
Lesson 23 Amazing teens 78
Lesson 24 In the spotlight 80
Get Connected 82
Review 84

Unit 7 Teen Time
Lesson 25 Teen opinions 86
Lesson 26 Unforgettable moments 88
Mini-review 90
Lesson 27 Are we alike? 92
Lesson 28 I'd rather 94
Get Connected 96
Review 98

Unit 8 Dreams and Reality
Lesson 29 Our dreams 100
Lesson 30 What would you do? ... 102
Mini-review 104
Lesson 31 What I'm going to be ... 106
Lesson 32 The past year 108
Get Connected 110
Review 112

Games 114

Get Connected Vocabulary Practice 122

Theme Projects 126

Verb List 134

Word List 138

Syllabus — Connect Student's Book 4

Unit 1 — My Life

Lesson	Function	Grammar	Vocabulary
Lesson 1 Last summer	Describing what you did last summer	Simple past and past continuous	Summer activities
Lesson 2 A new school year	Talking about plans for the new school year	*be going to*, *would like to*, *want to*, and *have to*	Classes, hobbies, and sports
Lesson 3 Life events	Describing life events and special accomplishments	*when* clauses of time + simple past	Life events
Lesson 4 Then and now	Describing past situations that have changed	*used to* and *not anymore*	Activities and physical descriptions
Get Connected	Reading • Listening • Writing		
Theme Project	Make a group booklet about people who make a difference.		

Unit 2 — The Future

Lesson	Function	Grammar	Vocabulary
Lesson 5 Predictions	Making predictions about the future	Future with *will* and *won't*	Future situations and actions
Lesson 6 When I'm older	Making guesses / predictions about the future	Future probability with *will probably / probably won't*	Life events
Lesson 7 Teen Center	Talking about activities at a Teen Center	Future possibility with *might / might not*	Activities offered at a Teen Center
Lesson 8 After high school	Talking about future plans	Definite plans with *will* and *be going to* / Probable plans with *will probably* / Possible plans with *might*	Life events
Get Connected	Reading • Listening • Writing		
Theme Project	Make a bookmark about your future.		

Unit 3 — Plans

Lesson	Function	Grammar	Vocabulary
Lesson 9 Weekend plans	Talking about weekend plans	*Would you like to . . . ?* for invitations	Weekend activities
Lesson 10 Evening plans	Asking permission and making requests	*Can / Could* for permission and requests	Evening activities
Lesson 11 Making plans	Talking about future plans	*if* with *will / will probably / won't / might*	Free-time activities
Lesson 12 Vacation plans	Talking about vacation plans	Clauses of time with *before / while / after*	Travel activities
Get Connected	Reading • Listening • Writing		
Theme Project	Make fact cards about an environmental issue.		

Unit 4 — People

Lesson	Function	Grammar	Vocabulary
Lesson 13 Teens online	Talking about activities teens enjoy	Gerunds as subjects / Gerunds as objects	Popular teen activities
Lesson 14 Personality types	Describing people's personalities	*too* / *either*	Personality descriptions
Lesson 15 Unusual people	Describing people's talents, habits, or collections	*who* clauses	Talents, habits, and collections
Lesson 16 Who's that girl?	Asking questions to confirm beliefs	Tag questions and answers with *be* / Tag questions and answers with the simple present	Describing people
Get Connected	Reading • Listening • Writing		
Theme Project	Make a group personality profile booklet.		

Unit 5 Entertainment	Lesson	Function	Grammar	Vocabulary
	Lesson 17 For fun	Describing activities done during the week	Present perfect with *I* and *We*	Everyday activities
	Lesson 18 Young entertainers	Describing someone's achievements	Present perfect with *he, she,* and *they*	Activities of famous people
	Lesson 19 Are you a fan?	Asking about past activities	Present perfect *Yes / No* questions with *ever*	Experiences
	Lesson 20 Pop culture trivia	Asking trivia questions about pop culture	*How long has / How long have . . . ?; since* and *for*	Pop culture
	Get Connected	Reading • Listening • Writing		
	Theme Project	Make a cross-cultural experiences poster.		

Unit 6 Experiences	Lesson	Function	Grammar	Vocabulary
	Lesson 21 Taking risks	Talking about new or risky activities	Present perfect with *never*	New or risky activities
	Lesson 22 What we've done	Talking about activities done in the past year	Simple past Present perfect	Interesting activities
	Lesson 23 Amazing teens	Talking about life events	*has already / hasn't . . . yet*	Life events
	Lesson 24 In the spotlight	Asking questions to confirm beliefs	Tag questions with the simple past and present perfect	Life events
	Get Connected	Reading • Listening • Writing		
	Theme Project	Make a booklet about amazing people.		

Unit 7 Teen Time	Lesson	Function	Grammar	Vocabulary
	Lesson 25 Teen opinions	Expressing opinions	*good / better / the best bad / worse / the worst*	Adjectives
	Lesson 26 Unforgettable moments	Talking about unforgettable moments	Superlative + *. . . have ever . . .*	Superlative adjectives
	Lesson 27 Are we alike?	Comparing people and their abilities	Formal and informal comparisons: *as . . . as / not as . . . as*	Adjectives to describe personality and abilities
	Lesson 28 I'd rather . . .	Talking about preferences	*would . . . rather* for preferences	Life preferences
	Get Connected	Reading • Listening • Writing		
	Theme Project	Make a poster about group preferences.		

Unit 8 Dreams and Reality	Lesson	Function	Grammar	Vocabulary
	Lesson 29 Our dreams	Talking about dreams and aspirations	*If* clauses with *could . . . would*	Dreams and aspirations
	Lesson 30 What would you do?	Talking about behavior in imagined situations	Unreal conditional with *if* clauses	Bad behavior
	Lesson 31 What I'm going to be	Talking about different professions	Infinitives to give a reason	Professions
	Lesson 32 The past year	Asking about life experiences	Indefinite pronouns	Interesting experiences
	Get Connected	Reading • Listening • Writing		
	Theme Project	Make a group booklet showing how you could help others with $5,000.		

Syllabus v

Lesson 1

Last summer

1 What did you do last summer?

A Read about the students at Wells International School. What did they do last summer? Listen and practice.

> Hi. I'm Jessica Chen. I'm from the U.S. I stayed at my grandparents' house near the beach last summer. One day, I met a girl from Colombia. We became great friends! We e-mail each other every day now.

> My name is Will Martins. I'm from New Zealand. I went camping with my friends. One day, when we were hiking, we got lost. We were afraid. Luckily, we had a compass, and we found our way back to the campground.

> Hi. My name is Juan Ramirez. I'm from Puerto Rico. I traveled all over Canada with my family. My favorite city was Toronto, but I liked Ottawa and Vancouver, too. When we were visiting the CN Tower, we saw a movie crew filming a movie. It was very exciting!

> Hello. I'm Carla Russo. I'm from Brazil. I went back to São Paulo – my hometown – for the summer. I hung out with my best friend a lot. We had a good time together. We went to some good movies. I was sad to leave São Paulo.

B Who did these things? Complete each sentence with *Jessica, Carla, Will,* or *Juan.*

1. _Juan_ took a family trip.
2. _____ visited grandparents.
3. _____ spent time with a best friend.
4. _____ got lost.
5. _____ made a new friend.
6. _____ went to a few different cities.

UNIT 1 My Life

2 Language focus review

Study the chart. Then complete the sentences about the other students, Pedro and Diana. Use the correct forms of the verbs. Then listen and check.

Simple past	Past continuous
Statements	**Statements**
I **went** camping. She **didn't do** anything else.	I **was eating** popcorn when the basketball hit me. She **wasn't studying** math.
Questions	**Questions**

What **did** you **do** last summer?
    I **went** to the beach.
Did he **go** to the beach?
    Yes, he **did**. / No, he **didn't**.
	What **was** she **studying**?
	    She **was making** her Web site. She **wasn't studying** English.
	Were they **having** fun?
	    Yes, they **were**. / No, they **weren't**.

1. Hi. I'm Pedro Domingo. I'm from Spain. My summer was OK. I ___took___ (take) tennis lessons, and I _____ (play) basketball. One day, I _____ (go) to watch a basketball game. I _____ (eat) popcorn when the basketball _____ (hit) me on the arm. It _____ (break) my arm! I _____ (not / play) tennis or basketball for the rest of the summer.

2. **Sue** This is Diana Martinez. She's from Ecuador. She has a twin brother. Last summer, she went to summer school.
   Brian What was she _____ (study)? _____ she _____ (study) English?
   Sue No, she _____ (not / be). She _____ (make) her own Web site. Diana _____ (work) on her Web site every day. She _____ (not / do) anything else. One day, when she _____ (put) pictures of Ecuador on her Web site, she _____ (get) an instant message from a boy in Italy. He _____ (want) to know about Ecuador.
   Brian Wow! How exciting.

3 Speaking

What did you do last summer? Answer the questions for yourself. Then ask a classmate the questions.

1. What did you do last summer? _____
2. Did anything interesting happen? _____

My Life   3

Lesson 2: A new school year

1 Language focus review

A Will and Carla talk about their plans for the new school year. Listen and practice.

Will So, do you have any special plans for this year?
Carla Yes. I'm going to join the drama club.
Will Really?
Carla Yeah. I'd like to act in the school play. How about you? Are you going to do anything special this year?
Will Well, I really want to learn to play the guitar, so I'm going to take music lessons. I'd love to play in a band someday.
Carla Wow, that's great.
Will And I'm going to study a lot this year. I have to get good grades.
Carla That's what *I* say every year!

B Study the chart. Complete the conversations with *(be) going to*, *(would) like to*, *want to*, or *have to*. Then listen and check.

be going to, would like to, want to, and have to		
Definite plans	**Hopes and wishes**	**Obligations**
I'**m going to** join the drama club.	I'**d like to** act in the school play. I **want to** learn to play the guitar.	I **have to** get good grades.

1. **Jessica** Hi, Juan. Are you _going to_ join the photography club this year?
   Juan I'd _____ join, but I can't. I _____ work at my uncle's restaurant after school. It's so boring.
   Jessica Oh, that's too bad. I'm _____ be a photographer for the school newspaper.

2. **Pedro** Hey, Diana. You're _____ take Mr. Bentley's science class, right?
   Diana Yes. I'd rather take a computer class, but I _____ take two science classes this year.
   Pedro I'd _____ take a computer class this year, too. I _____ design a computer game.

4 Unit 1

2 Listening

Jessica and Pedro talk about the new school year. Who talks about these things? Listen and check (✓) the correct boxes.

Who talks about . . . ?	Jessica	Pedro
studying French	☐	✓
playing on a sports team	☐	☐
joining a club	☐	☐
meeting new students	☐	☐
getting good grades	☐	☐
having free time	☐	☐

3 Word power

A Write these verb phrases in the correct columns. Then write two more verb phrases in each column.

- ☐ do gymnastics
- ☐ join a fan club
- ☐ study Web design
- ☐ do karate
- ☐ play volleyball
- ☐ take a computer course
- ✓ get good grades
- ☐ start a comic-book collection
- ☐ visit museums

Classes	Hobbies	Sports
get good grades		

B What are your plans for the year? Complete the sentences with the verb phrases in Part A or your own ideas.

1. I'm going to _____ this year.
2. I'd like to _____ this year.
3. I have to _____ this year.

4 Speaking

What are your classmates' plans for the new school year? Ask four classmates.

You What are your plans for the new school year, Jane?
Jane Well, I'm going to join the chess club. What are your plans?

My Life 5

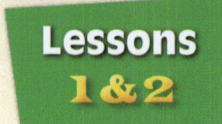

Lessons 1 & 2 Mini-review

1 Language check

A Jake and Tania are very busy at school this year. Complete the questions and write short answers.

1. **A** ___Did___ Jake and Tania join the chess club?
   B ___Yes, they did.___ They both love to play chess.
2. **A** _____ Jake join the volleyball team?
   B _____ Tania joined the volleyball team.
3. **A** _____ Jake have French club after school last Tuesday?
   B _____ He always studies French on Tuesday.
4. **A** _____ Tania practicing volleyball at 3:00 p.m. yesterday?
   B _____ We were all watching her.
5. **A** _____ Jake and Tania studying for the math test yesterday?
   B _____ He was practicing the guitar, and she was practicing the piano.
6. **A** _____ they pass the math test?
   B _____ They have too many extra activities. They have to study more.

B Check (✓) the correct words to complete the sentences.

1. **A** Are you taking Ms. Larson's geography class this year?
   B No. I'd like to take her class, but _____ to take Mr. Todd's history class this year.
   ☑ I have to ☐ I'd like to
2. **A** Are you going to take the computer course?
   B _____ take the course, but I don't have time.
   ☐ I'm going to ☐ I'd like to
3. **A** _____ do gymnastics this year. I love gymnastics.
   B Really? I don't like it at all. Gymnastics is too difficult for me.
   ☐ I want to ☐ I have to
4. **A** _____ start a stamp collection in my free time. I think stamps are cool.
   B That sounds like a good idea. Good luck!
   ☐ I'm going to ☐ I have to

6 Unit 1

C Read the newspaper article about fun things these students did last summer. Complete the sentences with the correct forms of the verbs. Use the simple past or the past continuous.

What did you do last summer?

1 My family and I _went_ (go) to amusement park on vacation. We _were waiting_ (wait) in line for a ride when I _____ (see) someone I knew in front of me. Guess who? Tina! She and her family _____ (visit) the park, too. So we _____ (spend) the day together there.

2 I _____ (go) camping for two weeks. We _____ (drive) to a campsite in the woods and _____ (put up) our tents. One night, we _____ (sleep) when a big storm _____ (start). We _____ (be) scared, and so we _____ (sleep) in the car that night. It was so uncomfortable that I _____ (wake up) with a sore back.

3 I _____ (have) a lot of fun at the city summer fair with my friends. We _____ (ride) on bumper cars, and we _____ (try) a lot of interesting foods. When the fireworks _____ (start), we _____ (eat) at a picnic table near the lake. The reflection of the fireworks on the water _____ (be) awesome!

4 My family and I _____ (take) a car trip. One day, we _____ (drive) down the highway when we _____ (see) a huge brown and white building in the shape of a cow. It _____ (be) a restaurant! We _____ (stop) and _____ (have) – what else? – ice cream. It was great!

2 Listening

🔘 What's next? Listen and check (✓) the correct responses.

1. ☑ I stayed home.
   ☐ I was watching TV.

2. ☐ Yes, I do. I like Spanish.
   ☐ Yes. I'm going to learn Spanish and French.

3. ☐ I'd like to join, but I have to take guitar lessons on Thursday.
   ☐ I was learning chess last year.

4. ☐ I was studying for the math test.
   ☐ I studied for the math test.

5. ☐ Yes, I do. I want to study a lot.
   ☐ Yes, I do. I want to join the photography club.

6. ☐ Yes, I was. I was traveling with my family.
   ☐ Yes, I did. I went on a trip with my family.

Go to page 114 for the Game.

My Life 7

Lesson 3: Life events

1 Language focus

A Read about people Carla, Pedro, and Will admire. Complete the sentences. Use *when* and the correct form of the verbs. Listen and check. Then practice.

> **when clauses of time + simple past**
>
> I joined a soccer team **when I was eight**.
> **When I was eight**, I joined a soccer team.
> ....
> I saw his concert **when he performed here**.
> **When he performed here**, I saw his concert.

Mia Hamm

1. I love everything about soccer. When I was eight, I joined a soccer team. I'd love to be like Mia Hamm someday. She won a World Cup championship when she was only 19. –Carla

Ryan Sheckler

2. Lang Lang is amazing. He _learned_ (learn) to play the piano _when_ he _was_ (be) only three years old. _____ he _____ (be) 13, he _____ (play) with an orchestra in Moscow. I love to play the piano, too. I _____ (see) Lang Lang's concert _____ he _____ (perform) in my town. It was incredible. –Pedro

Lang Lang

3. _____ I first _____ (see) Ryan Sheckler in a competition, I _____ (want) to be a champion skateboarder like him. He's the best in the world. Ryan _____ (be) only 18 months old _____ he _____ (find) his father's old skateboard and started to push it around. He became a professional at the age of 14. –Will

B Look at Carla's notes about soccer superstar Mia Hamm and complete the sentences. Then listen and check.

When Mia Hamm . . .		
was a young girl * moved a lot with her family * her parents gave her the nickname Mia	was a teenager * joined the U.S. National Team * played in her first World Cup match	was on the U.S. National Team * helped the team win Olympic gold medals * became famous

1. (young girl) When _Mia Hamm was a young girl, she moved a lot with her family_.
2. (young girl) _____ when _____.
3. (teenager) When _____, _____.
4. (teenager) _____ when _____.
5. (on the U.S. National Team) _____ when _____.
6. (famous) When _____,
_____.

8 Unit 1

2 Listening

Juan talks about events in his life. He is 15 years old now. When did these events happen? Was he a young boy or a teenager? Listen and check (✓) the correct boxes.

	Young boy	Teenager
1. learned to ride a horse	✓	☐
2. broke his leg	☐	☐
3. got a dog	☐	☐
4. cousin visited his school	☐	☐
5. joined a basketball team	☐	☐
6. moved to Ponce	☐	☐

3 Word power

A Create a verb phrase by adding a word or phrase from the box to each verb. Then check (✓) the things that you have done or experienced.

☐ American food   ☐ an award   ☐ a sports team   ☐ English   ✓ my leg
☐ a musical instrument   ☐ a pet   ☐ a trip   ☐ my best friend   ☐ the city

☐ broke _my leg_
☐ moved to _____
☐ learned to play _____
☐ learned _____
☐ met _____

☐ joined _____
☐ ate _____
☐ won _____
☐ went on _____
☐ got _____

B Write about events in your life. Use events from Part A or your own ideas.

When I fell off my bike, I broke my leg.
OR _I broke my leg when I fell off my bike._

1. _____
2. _____
3. _____
4. _____

4 Speaking

Share your events from Exercise 3B with your classmates. Answer their questions.

You When I fell off my bike, I broke my leg.
Classmate 1 How old were you?
You I was 12.

You I broke my leg when I fell off my bike.
Classmate 2 How old were you?
You I was 12.

My Life 9

Lesson 4: Then and now

1 Language focus

A What was Greg like when he was ten? Listen and practice.

Dave Is this you, Greg? You look so different!
Greg Yes. My friend took that picture when I was ten.
Dave You're so . . . thin now.
Greg Well, I used to be lazy, but I'm not anymore. Now I exercise every day.
Dave And your hair – it was so short!
Greg I know. I used to like short hair.
Dave And you wore glasses?
Greg Yes. I used to wear glasses, but I don't anymore. Now I wear contact lenses.
Dave You're a lot taller now, too.
Greg I know. I used to be the shortest person in my class, but I'm not anymore. Now I'm the tallest!

> **used to and not anymore**
>
> I **used to wear** glasses, but I **don't anymore**. Now I wear contact lenses.
>
> I **used to be** the shortest person in my class, but I**'m not anymore**. Now I'm the tallest.

B Look at the pictures. What did Greg use to do? What does he do now? Write sentences. Then listen and check.

7 years ago / Now

8 years ago

Now

1. (play) <u>He used to play video games, but he doesn't anymore. Now he plays soccer.</u>

2. (take) _____

4 years ago / Now

3 years ago / Now

3. (watch) _____

4. (wake up . . . on Saturdays) _____

10 Unit 1

2 Listening

How was Dave different when he was younger? Listen and complete the chart.

Topic	In the past	Now
Hobbies	collected comic books	collects stamps
Movies		
Sports		
Favorite subject		
Getting to school		

3 Pronunciation *used to*

A Listen. Notice how *used to* is reduced in conversation. Then listen again and practice.

I **used to** wear glasses.   He **used to** have short hair.

I **used to** play basketball.   He **used to** be shy.

B Now practice these sentences.

She **used to** play the violin, but she doesn't anymore.
They **used to** study French, but they don't anymore.
You **used to** be shy, but you're not anymore.

4 Speaking

A Think of yourself when you were a young child. What were you like? Complete the sentences with your own information.

I used to be _____.
I used to watch _____ on TV.
I used to play _____.
I used to wear _____.
I used to _____.
I used to _____.

B Now tell your classmates. Use your ideas from Part A.

> I used to be short, but I'm not anymore. Now I'm tall.

> I used to watch cartoons on TV. Now I watch music shows.

My Life   11

Get Connected
UNIT 1

Read

A Read the article quickly. Check (✓) the false statements.

☐ 1. Shawn Johnson is a top gymnast.
☐ 2. She started gymnastics when she was one year old.
☐ 3. She'd like to go back to Beijing and relax.

A Teenage Star

Gabrielle Douglas seems like an average girl. She likes to watch TV and listen to her favorite bands. She sings in the shower and she loves to dance. But Gabby isn't just *any* girl. She's an Olympic athlete, and has to **train** for five hours every day! While her friends were enjoying vacation last summer, she was traveling to the Olympic Games.

But how did this 4-foot, 9-inch teenager become a top **gymnast**? Well, Gabby learned the first moves from Arielle, her older sister. When she was 6, her mother took her to a gymnastics class. And Gabrielle loved it. When she was in elementary school, Gabby won her first state championship, and she never stopped. She moved away from her hometown and family at the age of 14 to train with a famous Olympic trainer.

She's the first American gymnast to win both individual and team gold at the same Olympics. She became one of America's **bestloved** sports stars! She also writes books. She says her newest publication is a **scrapbook** of her recent experiences. Now she's preparing for the next Olympics, while making time for seeing her family and friends in between.

Go to page 122 for the Vocabulary Practice.

B 🔘 Read the article slowly. Check your answers in Part A.

C Answer the questions.

1. Does Gabby have to train for five hours every week?
   <u>No, she doesn't. She has to train for four hours every day.</u>

2. What were Gabby's friends doing when she was competing?
   _____

3. What did Gabby's mother do when she was six?
   _____

4. What did she win at the Olympic Games?
   _____

5. What is Gabby doing at the moment?
   _____

We used to . . .

A 🔊 **Nick and Julie talk about swim team training. Listen and answer the questions.**

1. Did Julie answer Nick's phone calls? <u>No, she didn't.</u>
2. Why does the swim team have to train so hard? _____
3. Why are Julie's parents not too happy? _____
4. What would Julie like to be someday? _____
5. What are Nick and Julie going to do together? _____

B **What do you think? Answer the questions. Give reasons.**

1. Do you think doing one thing for three hours a day is too much?
   _____
2. Which is the most important: schoolwork, sports, or friends?
   _____
3. Would you like to be a teacher someday? _____
4. Do you think it's fun to play video games with friends? _____

Your turn

A **Think of a sport you have trained for or a hobby you have worked hard on. Answer the questions.**

1. What did you train for or work hard on? _____
2. How many hours a day did you train or work? _____
3. Why did you train or work? _____
4. What happened to your schoolwork and other activities? _____
5. Are you going to continue training or working hard? Why or why not?
   _____

B **Write a paragraph about your experience. Use the answers in Part A to help you.**

I . . .

My Life 13

Unit 1 Review

Language chart review

Simple past	Past continuous

What **did** you **do** yesterday?
  I **went** to the mall. I **didn't have** school yesterday.
Did your friends **go**, too?
  Yes, they **did**. / No, they **didn't**.
	What **was** Izzy **doing** yesterday?
	  She **was playing** video games. She **wasn't studying** history.
	Were you **studying** English?
	  Yes, we **were**. / No, we **weren't**.

when clauses of time + simple past

My friends gave me a surprise party **when I turned 13**.
When I got home, everyone said, "Surprise!"

A Complete the sentences with the simple past or the past continuous.

1. **Todd** I have a joke for you. A girl _was walking_ (walk) down the road when she _____ (see) three very large men. They _____ (stand) under a very small umbrella. There _____ (be) thunder and lightning, but the men didn't get wet.
   Sara Why not?
   Todd It _____ (not / rain)!

2. **Mona** I _____ (hear) a funny story today. There _____ (be) a class with a very scary teacher. Every day _____ (start) the same way. The teacher _____ (say), "Good morning, everyone." Then class _____ (begin). One day, when the teacher _____ (explain) the lesson, the door opened. The students _____ (look) up, but they _____ (not / see) anyone. When the teacher _____ (look) down, she _____ (see) Artie Sullivan, a student in her class. He was crawling on his hands and knees. "Why are you crawling into class, Artie?" the teacher _____ (ask). "On the first day of class, when you _____ (tell) us the classroom rules, you _____ (say), 'Never walk into my class late!' _____ (answer) Artie.

B Write questions to complete the conversation.

A _What did you do yesterday?_
B I bought some joke books yesterday.
A _____
B I bought the books at the mall.
A _____
B No, I didn't read them. I was studying all night.
A _____
B No, I wasn't studying English. I was studying history – the history of jokes.

14 Unit 1

Language chart review

be going to, would like to, want to, and have to

Definite plans: We**'re going to** play soccer after school today.
Hopes and wishes: I**'d like to** visit Japan someday.
I **want to** learn Japanese.
Obligations: We **have to** wear sneakers in the gym.

used to and not anymore

We **used to live** in an apartment, but we **don't anymore**. Now we have a house.

C Rewrite the sentences with *be going to, would like to, want to,* or *have to.* Change the meaning, using the ideas in parentheses.

1. I'd like to start my own fan club. (definite plan) *I'm going to start my own fan club.*

2. I'm going to make an exciting Web site for my club.
   a. (hope) _____
   b. (wish) _____

3. I want to work on the Web site today. (obligation) _____

4. I'd like to start a Jennifer Aniston fan club. (definite plan) _____

D Write sentences about what these people used to do and what they do now.

	Before	**Now**
1. Jennifer Lawrence	was a model	is an actor
2. Elijah Wood	acted in TV commercials	acts in movies
3. Johnny Depp	lived in the United States	lives in France
4. Beyoncé Knowles	sang with the group Destiny's Child	sings alone

1. *Jennifer Lawrence used to be a model, but she's not anymore. Now she's an actor.*
2. _____
3. _____
4. _____

Take another look!

Read the sentences. Circle the actions that happened first. Then underline the actions that happened second.

1. When Dad came home, we were watching TV.
2. When the phone rang, my mother answered it.

Go to page 126 for the Theme Project.

Lesson 5

Predictions

1 Language focus

A Read Professor Pete's Web site. Complete the predictions with *will* or *won't*. Listen and check. Then practice.

> **Future with *will* and *won't***
>
> Robots **will** help us.   **Will** robots cook?
> They**'ll** also clean.   **Yes,** they **will**.
> Robots **won't** replace humans.   **No,** they **won't**.
>
> I'll = I will   he'll = he will   we'll = we will
> you'll = you will   she'll = she will   they'll = they will
>
> won't = will not

Professor Pete's Predictions for 2030

1. Robots will help us in our homes. Will they cook? Yes, they will. They'll also clean and go shopping. But robots won't replace humans.

2. People _won't_ have to think about what to wear. "Smart" clothes _____ tell them if they look good or not.

3. Sleeping machines _____ help us sleep well. We _____ have bad dreams or nightmares. We _____ only have sweet dreams.

4. People _____ drive around the world on superhighways. The superhighways _____ connect the seven continents.

5. Students _____ stay in the classroom all the time. They _____ travel to space for their science class.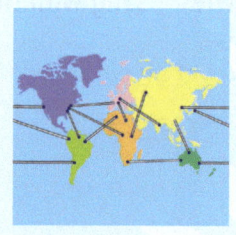

6. Schools _____ be open 24 hours a day. _____ students come to school at the same time every day? No, they _____.

B Which of Professor Pete's predictions do you think will come true? Ask a classmate. Use the first sentence of each prediction.

> What do you think? Will robots help us in our homes?

> Yes, they will. OR No, they won't.

UNIT 2 The Future

C Professor Pete has a new computer game about predictions. Complete the ad about his game with *will* or *won't*. Then listen and check.

Hey, kids! __Will__ computers replace humans someday? _____ everyone speak the same language? You _____ learn the answers to these questions when you play Professor Pete's new computer game. _____ you be bored? No, you _____. Professor Pete's game _____ entertain you for hours. Hurry and buy this game today. You _____ be sorry.

2 Listening

Two teens play Professor Pete's prediction game for 2030. Does Professor Pete agree with these predictions? Listen and check (✓) Agree or Disagree.

	Agree	Disagree
1. Students won't use paper and pencils in school.	✓	
2. Cell phones will be the size of a credit card.		
3. Most people won't shop in stores for food.		
4. People will stay on the moon on vacation.		
5. People will live below the sea.		

3 Speaking

A Write your own predictions for 2030. Use *will*.

	Predictions	Names
1. Robots		
2. Most people		
3. Students		
4. Movies		
5. Houses		
6. Cars		
7. TVs		

B Now find classmates who agree with your predictions. Write their names in the chart.

What do you think? Will robots do students' homework?

Yes, they will. OR No, they won't.

Lesson 6: When I'm older

1 Word power

A Match each verb phrase to its meaning. Then listen and practice.

1. be famous _d_
2. be rich ____
3. get a driver's license ____
4. get a job ____
5. get married ____
6. go to college ____
7. live alone ____
8. travel abroad ____

a. find a place to work
b. study after graduating from high school
c. not share your living space
d. have many people know who you are
e. visit a country far away from home
f. have a lot of money
g. pass a test to drive a car
h. become a husband or a wife

B What do you want to do or have happen before you are 25? Complete the sentences.

I want to _____ .
I want to _____ .
I want to _____ .
I want to _____ .

2 Language focus

A Jen and her father talk about the future. Listen and practice.

Jen Well, Dad, I probably won't be famous! I didn't win the singing competition at school today.

Mr. Wood That's OK, Jen. You have many other talents. You'll probably get a great job someday.

Jen Do you think so? I guess I *am* a good writer.

Mr. Wood Yes, you are. And you speak French well, too. You'll probably work for a French magazine someday.

Jen Gee. That sounds interesting. I'll also probably travel abroad . . . maybe to France.

Mr. Wood Anything is possible.

Jen And I'll probably get married to a handsome . . .

Mr. Wood OK, OK, Jen. Don't get too excited. You have to finish school first!

Jen Oh, I know. But it's good to have dreams, right?

B Study the chart. Then read about Jen's classmates. What do you think they will probably do in the future? Write sentences. Then listen and check.

Future probability with *will probably / probably won't*	
I'**ll probably** live abroad.	I **probably won't** be famous.
You'**ll probably** get a great job.	She **probably won't** be famous.

1. Max loves children. (have a big family) *He'll probably have a big family.*
2. Alicia isn't a star. (be famous) _____
3. Janet wants to study medicine. (go to college) _____
4. Kate and Dave don't like animals. (get a pet) _____
5. Emma doesn't like to drive. (get a driver's license) _____
6. George likes to read about different countries. (travel abroad) _____

3 Pronunciation Contracted form of *will*

A Listen. Notice how contracted forms of *will* are pronounced. Then listen again and practice.

I **will** probably travel to England.	I'**ll** probably travel to England.
She **will** probably be a good writer.	She'**ll** probably be a good writer.

B Practice the sentences you wrote in Exercise 2B.

4 Speaking

Write four things you will probably do or probably won't do before you are 25. Use the cues in Exercise 1B or your own ideas. Tell your classmates.

1. _____
2. _____
3. _____
4. _____

I'll probably travel abroad. I probably won't get married.

The Future   19

Lessons 5 & 6

Mini-review

1 Language check

A Look at the pictures from a class yearbook. Then write two sentences about each person. Use *will probably* and *probably won't*.

1 Ben Taylor
Ben is a great guitar player. He doesn't like to study.

2 Cho Park
Cho loves children. She doesn't like to travel abroad.

3 Javier Lopez
Javier doesn't like drama class. He loves cars.

4 Carolyn Davis
Carolyn doesn't like animals. She's a very good student.

5 Lucy Romero
Lucy likes to write. She doesn't like the news.

6 Bert Talbot
Bert doesn't like school. He likes to cook.

1. Ben (be a famous rock star / go to college)
   <u>Ben will probably be a famous rock star.</u>
   <u>He probably won't go to college.</u>

2. Cho (become a teacher / go to Spain on vacation)
   _____
   _____

3. Javier (become an actor / get his driver's license next year)
   _____
   _____

4. Carolyn (get a cat or a dog / win a prize at graduation)
   _____
   _____

5. Lucy (write books / work for a news magazine)
   _____
   _____

6. Bert (be a teacher / open a restaurant)
   _____
   _____

B Read these interesting predictions students put on the Internet. Complete the texts with the correct forms of *will* and *won't*.

Our Favorite Predictions from the Internet

1. People __won't__ use money or credit cards anymore. Special machines _____ read our fingerprints. We _____ pay for things that way. —Lisa

2. We _____ have to type on computers. Instead, we _____ say the words, and the computer _____ type them. —Andrea

3. Cars _____ drive themselves. We _____ just tell the cars where to go. So kids my age _____ be able to drive. —Sam

4. I _____ have a pet robot dog. I _____ have to feed it, and I _____ have to walk it. The dog _____ only need batteries! —Justin

5. People _____ live longer, and they _____ be active longer. People _____ get sick anymore. There _____ be many more ways to cure sickness. —Grace

2 Listening

Students talk about other predictions. Does Kim agree or disagree with these predictions? Listen and check (✓) the correct boxes.

	Agree	Disagree
1. People will travel from place to place in small airplanes.	☐	☐
2. People will take their houses with them when they move.	☐	☐
3. People won't need to learn foreign languages.	☐	☐
4. People won't need to cook.	☐	☐

Go to page 115 for the Game.

Lesson 7 Teen Center

1 Word power

A What activities are these students going to do at the Teen Center? Listen and practice.

1. Join the marching band.
2. Be a reporter.
3. Take martial arts classes.
4. Learn how to edit a music video.
5. Take ballroom dancing classes.
6. Learn how to make a scrapbook.
7. Take cooking classes.
8. Join the racket club.
9. Be a recreation leader.

B Write each activity in Part A next to the correct description.

1. Students will need their own video cameras. *Learn how to edit a music video.*
2. Learn how to make all kinds of food. _____
3. Learn the rumba and the samba. Please sign up with a partner. _____
4. Learn karate and judo with your friends. _____
5. Be in the school parade. Play in competitions. _____
6. Play tennis and badminton. Beginner students are welcome. _____
7. Write articles for the school newspaper. _____
8. Bring your favorite photos to class. _____
9. Play games with young children. Have fun. _____

22 Unit 2

2 Language focus

> **Future possibility with *might* / *might not***
>
> My friends and I **might** take ballroom dancing classes.
> I **might not** have time.
>
> *I might = maybe I'll*

A Pam and Marla talk about what they will do at the Teen Center. Listen and practice.

Pam Hi, Marla. Are you going to sign up for any activities at the Teen Center?
Marla Sure. I'm trying to decide what to do.
Pam Me, too. My friends and I might take ballroom dancing classes, but I'm really busy this year. I might not have time.
Marla I want to do something new this year. I'm not sure what to do. I might take martial arts classes or be a reporter for the center's newspaper.
Pam Hmm. I'd like to help out at the center. I might be a recreation leader. They play games with young kids. Why don't you do that, too? We can work together.
Marla Well, I'm not very good with young children.
Pam Oh, sure you are, Marla. It'll be a lot of fun.

B Juan writes an e-mail to his friend Mark. What might he do this year? Complete the sentences with *might* or *might not*. Then listen and check.

> Hi, Mark!
>
> How are you? I'm fine. This year is going to be fun. I'm going to do some things at the Teen Center. I'm not sure what I'll do. I ___might___ take martial arts classes, or I _____ learn how to edit a music video. I'd like to take ballroom dancing classes, but I don't have a partner. I'm shy, but I _____ ask another student to join me. I'd like to ask Diana, but she's really busy, so she _____ have time.
>
> Next week, I'm also going to be very busy – with school! I won't have a lot of free time, so I _____ e-mail you. Anyway, have a great week.
>
> –Juan

3 Listening

Listen to the conversations. Who might do the activities? Who might not? Write *might* or *might not* for each student.

1. take cooking classes   Amy   ___might___   Sam   ___might not___
2. join the marching band   José   _____   Anna   _____
3. learn how to edit a music video Staci _____   John   _____
4. learn how to make a scrapbook Felicia _____ Laura _____
5. be a reporter   Paul   _____   James _____

Lesson 8: After high school

1 Language focus

A What are these students' plans after high school? Match the first sentence to the rest of the text. Then listen and practice.

Simon, 15, China
I'll travel for a couple of months. ___

Moira, 17, Ireland
After high school, I'm going to go to college. ___

Andrea, 16, Argentina
I won't go to college right after high school. ___

1 I'm going to get a job and make some money. I might get a job at an international hotel. I'll probably have to use my English.

2 I'll go with two friends. We'll probably go to the U.S. and Canada first. If we have time, we might backpack around Europe.

3 I'll probably go to City College. I might study computer programming, or I might study history. I can't decide.

B Study the chart. Then read the statements. Check (✓) D (definite plans) or P (probable / possible plans). Then listen and check.

Definite plans with *will* and *be going to* / Probable plans with *will probably* / Possible plans with *might*

I**'ll** travel for a couple of months.	We**'ll probably** go to the U.S.
I**'m going to** go to college.	I **might** study computer programming.

	D	P
1. Simon is going to take a trip.	✓	☐
2. Simon will travel with friends.	☐	☐
3. Simon will probably visit the U.S.	☐	☐
4. Moira will go to college.	☐	☐
5. Moira might study computer programming.	☐	☐
6. Andrea will make some money.	☐	☐
7. Andrea will probably use her English.	☐	☐
8. Andrea might work at a hotel.	☐	☐

C Will and Diana talk about their plans after high school. Complete the conversation with *will*, *(be) going to*, *I'll probably*, or *might*. Then listen and check.

Will So, what are you _going to_ do after high school?
Diana Well, first I'm _____ take a long vacation.
Will _____ you go to college someday?
Diana Yes, definitely. What are you _____ do after high school?
Will I'm not sure. I _____ go to college, or I _____ visit Spain. So _____ take Spanish lessons.
Diana Great! I can help you with Spanish. How are you _____ pay for the lessons?
Will Well, my dad is very busy in his store. _____ help him. He's _____ pay me.
Diana Great idea! I really need money, too. I'm _____ ask my mom if I can help her with chores at home. She _____ pay me. I hope so.

2 Word power

Write the verb phrases in the correct columns. Then write one more verb phrase in each column.

- ☐ get a job
- ☐ go around the world
- ☑ go to college
- ☐ make money
- ☐ see the U.S.
- ☐ study computer programming
- ☐ take English classes
- ☐ take a trip to Europe
- ☐ work in an office

School	Travel	Work
go to college		

3 Speaking

What are you going to do after high school? Complete the sentences with the verb phrases from Exercise 2 or your own ideas. Then share your plans with three classmates.

1. I'm going to _____ .
2. I'm not going to _____ .
3. I might _____ .
4. I'll probably _____ .
5. I'll _____ .
6. I won't _____ .

Get Connected
UNIT 2

Read

A Read the Web site quickly. Check (✓) one thing the Web site does *not* talk about.

☐ a flying car ☐ electricity from the sun ☐ newspapers
☐ medicines   ☐ virtual reality glasses

An Exciting Future

"First **Flying** Car Made," say the newspaper **headlines**! Do we have flying cars today? No, we don't. But in the future, that might be a newspaper headline. However, we probably won't have newspapers in the future. We'll get all our news on video cell phones.

So what will our world look like 10, 20, or 50 years from now? One Web site makes predictions about the future and writes articles about the future. Its prediction for August 23, 2025, reads: *The first hotel on the moon finally opens*. But predictions about the future are difficult. Will people go to the moon for their vacations? They might. Will we find new **medicines** and **cure** terrible sicknesses? We probably will. Will our homes use electricity from the sun and wind? Yes, they will. And *we* won't clean our houses – robots will do this – and cars won't need **gas** anymore.

We don't know these things for sure. But one thing is **certain** . . . our lives in the future will be different from now. And that's very exciting!

Go to page 122 for the Vocabulary Practice.

B Read the Web site slowly. Check your answer in Part A.

C Circle the correct words to complete the sentences or the correct answers.

1. In the future we probably won't have (newspapers / video cell phones / new medicines).

2. A headline for 2025 predicts we will have (flying cars / terrible sicknesses / hotels on the moon).

3. In the future our homes will get electricity from (the sun and wind / the moon / robots).

4. In the future we won't (drive our cars / clean our homes / use medicines).

5. Will our lives be different in the future? (Yes, probably. / No. Not at all. / Yes, they will.)

26 Unit 2

Computers will . . .

A 🎧 Rosa and Jeff talk about the future. Listen and write *True* or *False*. Then correct the false statements.

1. Rosa wants to go to the movies with Jeff.
   True. _____

2. Jeff and Rosa think that robots won't do students' homework in the future. _____ _____

3. A magazine article says that computers won't be amazing.
   _____ _____

4. In the future computers will type what people are thinking.
   _____ _____

5. Someday people will connect computers to their brains.
   _____ _____

B What do you think? Answer the questions. Give reasons.

1. Would you like robots to do anything for you? What? _____
2. Do you think computers will be smarter than people? _____
3. Do you think computers will be able to type what we are thinking in the future?
   _____
4. Would you like to connect a computer to your brain? _____

Your turn

A What do you think the future will be like? Write *clothes*, *computers*, *food*, *houses*, or *schools* to start a web about your own predictions.

B Write an article about your future predictions. Use the web in Part A to help you.

In the future, . . .

The Future 27

Unit 2 Review

Language chart review

Future with *will* and *won't*

Robots **will** be very smart.
They**'ll** be powerful.
They **won't** think for us.
Will robots have feelings?
　Yes, they **will**. / **No**, they **won't**.

Future probability with *will probably* / *probably won't*

I**'ll probably** drive a small car.
I **probably won't** ride a bicycle.

Future possibility with *might* / *might not*

I **might** work at Leo's Drugstore this year.
I **might not** have much free time.

A Look at the pictures. Write sentences with the verb phrases in the box.
Use *probably* or *might* to make guesses about future probability.

- ☐ drink the milk / drink orange juice
- ☐ go out in those shoes / wear her other shoes
- ☐ go to the movie / go to a café
- ☑ ride his bike / walk to school

1. *He won't ride his bike. He'll probably walk to school.*

2. _____

3. _____

4. _____

B Look at the pictures in Part A again. Write questions with *will*. Then answer the questions.

1. he / fix the bike
   Q: Will he fix the bike?
   A: Yes, he will.

2. they / drink the milk
   Q: _____
   A: _____

3. they / go to a café
   Q: _____
   A: _____

4. she / wear other shoes
   Q: _____
   A: _____

Language chart review

> **Definite plans with *will* and *be going to* / Probable plans with *will probably* / Possible plans with *might***
>
> I**'ll study** tomorrow night. I**'m going to** stay up late.
> They**'ll probably** travel together.
> We **might** spend a week in Rio.

C Match the two parts of each sentence to complete the conversation.

A What are you going to do c
B I'll probably go ____
A Do you think you'll be ____
B I don't think I'll make ____
A At what age do you think you'll get ____
B I might not get ____

a. a lot of money.
b. married at all.
c. after high school?
d. rich and famous?
e. to college to study medicine.
f. married?

D Write the questions from Part C. Then answer them with your own information.

1. **Q:** What are you going to do after high school?
   A: _____
2. **Q:** _____
   A: _____
3. **Q:** _____
   A: _____

Take another look!

Circle the correct answers.

1. Which sentence means the same as "I might learn French"?
   a. Maybe I'll learn French.   b. I'm going to learn French.
2. Which sentence talks about definite plans?
   a. I might not go swimming.   b. I won't go swimming.

Go to page 127 for the Theme Project.

Lesson 9: Weekend plans

1 Word power

A Match each verb or verb phrase to its meaning. Then listen and practice.

1. amaze _f_
2. come back ____
3. expect ____
4. explore ____
5. head for ____
6. rescue ____
7. take off ____
8. try out ____

a. think that something will happen
b. travel around a place to learn about it
c. return
d. test something by using it
e. leave the ground and start flying
f. surprise very much
g. save someone in danger
h. move toward a place

B Complete the description of each weekend event with a pair of verbs or verb phrases in the box.

- ☐ expect / try out
- ☑ explore / rescue
- ☐ head for / amaze
- ☐ take off / come back

① Go on a cave tour!

You can spend an exciting hour here! You can _explore_ one of many caves. You'll probably see bats, and you might get lost. But don't worry, we'll _rescue_ you.

Friday and Saturday
9:00 a.m. – 10:00 p.m.
Carl's Caves

② See a circus show!

At 2:00 p.m., _____ the Big City Circus Tent and see the Flying Vitale Family. They will _____ you as they fly through the air on the trapeze.

Saturday and Sunday
2:00 p.m. and 8:00 p.m.
Big City Circus Tent

③ Visit Futureland!

Come to the grand opening of Futureland. Try our newest virtual reality ride – Rocket Ship. You'll _____ , visit the moon, and never want to _____ .

Sunday
9:00 a.m. – 11:00 p.m.
Futureland

④ Drive go-carts!

You can _____ an exciting ride at Go-Carts Galore. First drive the latest go-carts on our superfast track. After that, you can _____ our three brand-new racing tracks.

Saturday
4:00 p.m. to 9:00 p.m.
Go-Carts Galore

2 Language focus

A Nina invites Becky to go on the cave tour. Listen and practice.

> **Would you like to . . . ? for invitations**
>
> **Would you like to** go on a cave tour?
> Accepting: **Yes, I'd love to.**
> **Sure, I'd like to.**
> Refusing: **I'm sorry, but I can't. I have to** babysit.
> **I'd love to, but I can't.**

Nina Hi, Becky. Would you like to go on the cave tour with me on Saturday morning?
Becky Oh, Saturday morning? I'm sorry, but I can't. I have to babysit my little sister.
Nina Well, would you like to go in the afternoon instead?
Becky Sure, I'd like to. But, uh, there might be bats in the cave. They're scary.
Nina There are *supposed* to be bats in a cave! Come on, Becky. It'll be fun.
Becky Well, OK. Oh! I almost forgot. My family is going to see the Flying Vitale Family on Sunday afternoon. Would you like to go with us?
Nina Wow! Yes, I'd love to. We're going to have a great weekend. I can't wait.

B Write invitations to the events in Exercise 1B. Use the responses as clues. Then listen and check.

1. <u>Would you like to see the circus show?</u>
   Yes, I'd love to. The Flying Vitale Family is amazing.

2. _____
   Sure, I'd like to. I like fast and exciting things.

3. _____
   Yes, I'd love to. I want to try the Rocket Ship.

C Now refuse invitations 2 and 3 in Part B. Use different expressions.

1. _____
2. _____

3 Speaking

Invite classmates to do things with you this weekend. Write three invitations. Then find a classmate who accepts each invitation.

1. _____
2. _____
3. _____

You Would you like to go to a movie on Saturday afternoon?
Classmate 1 I'm sorry, but I can't. I have to study for a test.
You Would you like to go to a movie on Saturday afternoon?
Classmate 2 Sure, I'd love to.

Lesson 10: Evening plans

1 Language focus

A Matt asks his mom some favors. Listen and practice.

Matt Hey, Mom. Could you buy me a new digital camera today? Mine is broken, and Alex wants me to take pictures at his party tonight.
Mrs. Hays No, I'm sorry. I can't, Matt.
Matt Oh, Mom. Well, can I stay out until 10:00?
Mrs. Hays Yes, all right. But be home at 10:00 sharp!
Matt OK. And, uh, can John sleep over after the party?
Mrs. Hays Sure, that's fine. But we have to get up early, remember? We're going to go visit Aunt Becky.
Matt Oh, yes! I forgot. And, um, Mom, could you lend me $15?
Mrs. Hays $15? No, I can't. Sorry.

B Study the chart. Complete the questions with *Can I* or *Could you*. Then listen and check.

Can / Could for permission and requests	
Asking permission	**Making requests**
Can I stay out until 10:00? Yes, all right. / No, I'm sorry. **Can John** sleep over? Sure, that's fine.	**Could you** buy me a digital camera? No, I'm sorry. I can't. **Could you** lend me $15? Yes, of course. / No, I can't. Sorry.
Note: Young children often use *can* for both permission and requests. *Can* may be used for requests, but it is less formal.	

1. _Can I_ borrow your favorite shirt?
2. _____ buy me a pet for my birthday?
3. _____ stay out late on Friday?
4. _____ clean my room, please?
5. _____ go to the movies this weekend?
6. _____ sleep over at Ken's house tonight?
7. _____ make my bed?

C Read the survey. Which of the four responses would your parents give to each question? Complete the chart. Then total the points. Are your parents easygoing, average, or strict?

Yes, of course. (1 point)   No, I'm sorry. (3 points)
Maybe. Let me think about it. (2 points)   Absolutely not. (4 points)

	Response	Points
1. Can I have a party at home this weekend?		
2. Can I watch TV tonight?		
3. Can I use your new tablet?		
4. Can I go downtown with my friends now?		
5. Could you help me with my homework?		
6. Can I stay out until midnight tomorrow?		
7. Can I buy an electric guitar?		
8. Could you lend me $20?		

Total points:

My parents are:
☐ easygoing (8–16 points)   ☐ average (17–24 points)   ☐ strict (25–32 points)

2 Pronunciation *Could you*

A Listen. Notice how *Could you* is reduced in conversation. Then listen again and practice.

Could you close the door, please?   **Could you** lend me some money?

Could you help me?   **Could you** bring me some water, please?

B Now practice the *Could you* questions in Exercises 1B and 1C.

3 Listening

A Some teens talk to their parents. Are they asking permission or making requests? Listen and check (✓) Permission or Request.

	Permission	Request
1.	☐	☐
2.	☐	☐
3.	☐	☐
4.	☐	☐

B Listen again. Do their parents say yes or no? Write *Yes* or *No*.

1. _____   2. _____   3. _____   4. _____

Lessons 9 & 10 Mini-review

1 Language check

A Match the questions to the correct responses.

1. Would you like to go out to eat? _c_
2. Could you help me make dinner? ____
3. Would you like to play chess? ____
4. Can I go to the mall tonight? ____
5. Could you order a pizza? ____

a. Yes, all right. But be back by 9:00.
b. Sure. What's the phone number?
c. I'm sorry, but I can't. I just ate.
d. Yes. I'll cut the vegetables.
e. I'd love to, but I can't. I don't know how to play.

B Write questions. Use the verb phrases in the box and *Would you like to, Can I,* or *Could you.*

- ☑ borrow your bike
- ☐ go shopping at the mall
- ☐ help me with this math problem
- ☐ come to my party
- ☐ have a cookie
- ☐ lend me your skateboard

1. **Q:** *Can I borrow your bike?*
   A: Yes, of course. But give it back to me tomorrow.

2. **Q:** _____
   A: Absolutely not. I want to go skateboarding today.

3. **Q:** _____
   A: Thanks. I'd love to come. Do you want me to bring anything?

4. **Q:** _____
   A: Sure. Show it to me.

5. **Q:** _____
   A: No, I can't. Sorry. I have to finish my homework.

6. **Q:** _____
   A: I'd love to. They look delicious.

C Read the invitations. Accept or refuse each one. Use a different answer each time.

1. **Q:** Would you like to study English with me tonight?
   A: _____

2. **Q:** Would you like to go swimming with me on Saturday?
   A: _____

3. **Q:** Would you like to go to the movies this weekend?
   A: _____

4. **Q:** Would you like to run in the park with me tomorrow?
   A: _____

34 Unit 3

D Write conversations for these situations.

1. You ask your father for permission to go hiking on Saturday. Your father says yes, and to have a good time.

    Q: <u>Can I go hiking on Saturday?</u>

    A: <u>Sure, that's fine. Have a good time.</u>

2. You ask your mother for permission to go to your friend Angelo's house after school. She says no because you have to practice for your piano lesson.

    Q: _____

    A: _____

3. You ask a friend to help you with your math homework. Your friend says yes and suggests going to the library.

    Q: _____

    A: _____

4. You ask a friend to lend you his bike. He says no because his bike is broken.

    Q: _____

    A: _____

2 Listening

A Listen to the conversations. Are the people in the conversations offering an invitation, asking permission, or making a request? Check (✓) the correct answers.

	Invitation	Permission	Request
1.	✓	☐	☐
2.	☐	☐	☐
3.	☐	☐	☐
4.	☐	☐	☐

B Listen again and answer the questions.

1. Can David go to the museum?

    <u>No, he can't.</u>

2. Does Billy have to take the history test today?

    _____

3. Will Sally clean Alex's room?

    _____

4. Would Miranda like to go white-water rafting?

    _____

Go to page 116 for the Game.

Lesson 11: Making plans

1 Language focus

A Pedro and Juan make plans for the next day. Listen and practice.

> **if with will / will probably / won't / might**
>
> **If** the weather is nice, **I'll** ride in the park.
> **If** it doesn't rain, we**'ll probably** go to the beach.
> We **might** go to the movies **if** it rains.
> I **won't** ride my bike **if** it rains.

Pedro So, Juan, what are you going to do tomorrow?
Juan I really want to go for a ride on my new bike. If the weather is nice, I'll ride in the park. How about you? Do you have any plans?
Pedro I'm going to hang out with my cousin, David.
Juan What are you and David going to do?
Pedro Well, I'm not sure. It depends on the weather. If it doesn't rain, we'll probably go to the beach.
Juan And if it rains?
Pedro We might go to the movies if it rains. Would you like to join us?
Juan I'd love to. I won't ride my bike if it rains.
Pedro Good. But I hope it's sunny. I really want to go to the beach.

B Complete the sentences with the correct forms of the verbs. Then listen and check.

1. If the Larsons _don't go_ (not go) to the concert, they _'ll probably stay_ (probably stay) home.
2. If it _____ (rain) on the weekend, Kelly _____ (not play) tennis.
3. _____ (I / be) in the library if you _____ (need) my help.
4. If Nick _____ (run), he _____ (might / not be) late for class.
5. We _____ (might / eat) at an outdoor café if it _____ (be) sunny on Sunday.
6. If I _____ (not have) extra money, I _____ (not buy) your ticket.
7. If we _____ (not have) time tonight, we _____ (do) it tomorrow.
8. They _____ (probably / not walk) to school if it _____ (not be) warm.

36 Unit 3

2 Word power

A Which activities are good for a sunny day? Which are good for a rainy day? Write the verb phrases in the correct columns. Then write one more verb phrase in each column.

- ✓ play computer games
- ☐ fly a kite
- ☐ have a barbecue
- ☐ go to an outdoor concert
- ☐ rent a DVD
- ☐ go biking
- ☐ clean my room
- ☐ visit a museum

Activities for a sunny day	Activities for a rainy day
	play computer games

B Imagine you have a free day tomorrow. What will you do? Complete the sentences with ideas from Part A or your own ideas.

1. If it doesn't rain tomorrow, _____.
2. If I go downtown on Saturday, _____.
3. _____ if it rains in the morning.
4. If I have some extra money, _____.
5. _____ if we don't have any homework today.
6. If I stay home, _____.
7. If I'm not tired tonight, _____.
8. _____ if my friend isn't busy tomorrow.

3 Speaking

Look at Exercise 2B. What are your plans for your free day? Find a classmate who has the same plans as you.

You If it doesn't rain, I'll go to the beach. How about you?
Classmate 1 If it doesn't rain, I might play volleyball.

You If it doesn't rain, I'll go to the beach. How about you?
Classmate 2 If it doesn't rain, I'll go to the beach, too.

Plans 37

Lesson 12: Vacation plans

1 Language focus

A Jessica is going on vacation. Read her e-mail message to Will. Then listen and practice.

Clauses of time with *before* / *while* / *after*
Before I go, I have a lot to do.
While I'm in Hawaii, I'm going to have fun.
I'm going to go to the beach **while** I'm there.
Let's get together **after** I get back.

Hi, Will!

I'm so excited. I'm going to Hawaii tomorrow. Can you believe it?

Before I go, I have a lot to do. I have to finish my book report before I go! It's OK, because while I'm in Hawaii, I'm going to have fun. There are so many things to do on the island of Oahu. I'm going to go to the beach with my cousin while I'm there. She'll probably take me sightseeing, too. And we'll snorkel at Hanauma Bay after I buy some snorkel gear.

I hope you have a great vacation. Let's get together after I get back.

Take care!
Jessica

B Match the two parts of each sentence. Then listen and check.

1. Before I leave, _d_
2. I'm going to pack my bags ____
3. While I'm there, ____
4. I'll take lots of pictures ____
5. I'll call you ____

a. after I get back.
b. while I'm there.
c. I'll probably take surfing lessons.
d. I might stop by to say good-bye.
e. before I go to bed tonight.

C Imagine you are going on vacation. Complete the sentences with your own information.

1. Before I leave, I might _____ .
2. I'll _____ before I leave.
3. I'll probably _____ while I'm there.
4. While I'm there, I'm going to _____ .
5. I might _____ after I get back.

2 Listening

Carla is going on vacation to Disney World with her family. When will she do these things? Listen and check (✓) the correct columns.

	Before she leaves	While she's there	After she gets home
1. buy a camera	✓	☐	☐
2. go shopping	☐	☐	☐
3. get a haircut	☐	☐	☐
4. read a travel book	☐	☐	☐
5. write postcards	☐	☐	☐
6. call her friend	☐	☐	☐

3 Speaking

A Choose one of the vacations below. Then complete the chart.

a beach vacation

a cruise

a country tour

a ski vacation

Vacation Planner

I'm going to take _____.

What are you going to do . . . ?

before you leave	when you arrive	while you are there
_____	_____	_____
_____	_____	_____

if the weather is bad	after you get home
_____	_____
_____	_____

B Tell a classmate about your vacation plans.

> I'm going to take a ski vacation. Before I leave, I'm going to buy ski pants.

Get Connected
UNIT 3

Read

A Read the article quickly. Check (✓) the main idea.

☐ 1. Teenagers are very social these days.

☐ 2. Teenagers make plans with their friends after school because it's convenient.

☐ 3. Most teenagers use modern technology for their social plans.

WAYD 2nite?

What do you do when you want to go out with your friends? Do you call them on your phone? Maybe. But these days, most teenagers use their phones for **texting**, and they'll probably text this message: *WAYD 2nite?* (What are you doing tonight?) Texting is very **convenient**. You can send messages from the mall, the bus – anywhere.

Teens also like to go online to make plans. They often send **e-vites** – electronic invitations – or use **social networking Web sites**. On Web sites like these, you can make plans with all your friends at the same time.

You can make **fuzzy** plans (plans that might happen), like: "If the weather is nice, I'll probably go to the park," or "We might go to the movies tonight if class doesn't finish late." You can also make **firm** plans (plans that will happen), like: "I'm going to the zoo on Saturday. Do you want to come?" If your friends go on the site, they'll see your plans. They might send you a reply online, or text you a short reply. For example: *XLNT idea* (Excellent idea). Or *IMS 2BZ* (I'm sorry. I'm too busy).

Go to page 123 for the Vocabulary Practice.

B Read the article slowly. Check your answer in Part A.

C Are these statements true or false? Write *True* or *False*. Then correct the false statements.

1. A lot of teenagers use texting for their social plans. _True._

2. Texting isn't convenient when you're on the bus or at the mall. _____

3. E-vites are invitations you send online. _____

4. Fuzzy plans are plans that won't happen. _____

5. Friends can't reply to your online plans. _____

Can you come to my party?

Listen

A Olivia and Carlos talk about texting and technology. Listen and answer the questions.

1. Why does Olivia ask Carlos for help?
   <u>She can't understand the text messages on her phone.</u>
2. What does Carlos say to Olivia about learning texting?
   _____
3. Does Olivia think technology is wonderful?
   _____
4. Do Olivia and Carlos agree that technology is convenient?
   _____
5. Does Olivia spend more time doing homework or learning technology?
   _____

B What do you think? Write *I agree*, *I disagree*, or *I'm not sure*. Give reasons.

1. People should talk face-to-face more. _____
2. I think technology is convenient and fun. _____
3. New technology can be difficult to learn. _____
4. Technology makes the world a better place. _____

Your turn

Write

A How important is technology in your life? Answer the questions. Give reasons.

1. How often do you use technology? _____
2. What's your favorite way to keep in touch with friends? _____
3. Do you use a social networking site? _____
4. How often do you text your friends? _____
5. Is it easy for you to learn how to use new technology? _____

B Write a paragraph about technology in your life. Use the answers in Part A to help you.

I use my . . .

Unit 3 Review

Language chart review

Would you like to . . . ? for invitations	Can / Could for permission and requests	
	Asking permission	Making requests

Would you like to see a movie?
  Yes, I'd love to. / Sure, I'd like to.
  I'm sorry, but I can't. / I'd love to,
    but I can't. **I have to** clean my room.
	Can I use your pen?
	  Yes, all right.
	  No, I'm sorry.
		Could you give me a pen?
		  Yes, of course.
		  No, I can't. Sorry.

Clauses of time with *before / while / after*

Before he goes to bed, he has to take out the trash.
While I'm at the mall, I'm going to look for some T-shirts.
They'd like to see that movie **after it comes out on DVD**.

A Mario and his dad are talking. Complete their conversation with *would you like to*, *can I*, and *could you*.

Mario <u>Can I</u> have a birthday party this year?
Dad Sure. _____ have the party next Saturday?
Mario Yes, I'd love to. _____ invite all my friends?
Dad OK. How many friends? _____ give me an idea?
Mario Yes, of course. There's Marisa, Gavin, Brenda, Min-ho, and Ashton. And _____ invite some other friends from school, too?
Dad Yes, all right. _____ have the party here, or somewhere else?
Mario Here. _____ start calling everyone now?
Dad Everyone?

B Mario is planning his party. Write sentences.

1. have to do a lot / before / his friends arrive
   <u>Mario has to do a lot before his friends arrive.</u>

2. before / Mario's friends play games / eat dinner
   _____

3. while / eat dinner / his friends talk
   _____

4. his friends / dance / after / eat dessert
   _____

Language chart review

if with will / will probably / won't / might

If I have homework, I'll do it after dinner.
They'll probably go biking if they don't have homework.

We might go to a movie if we have time.
I won't go to school if I'm sick.

C Mario's friends are at his party. They are playing the "If" game. Complete their sentences with the correct forms of the verbs.

1. **Ashton** I'll go first! If Pandora, my favorite band, ___comes___ (come) to our town, ___they'll probably play___ (they / probably play) at the stadium.
2. **Min-ho** If Pandora _____ (play) at the stadium, Ashton _____ (go) to the concert.
3. **Brenda** He _____ (might / buy) tickets if he _____ (have) some extra money.
4. **Mario** If Marisa _____ (go) to the concert, she'll _____ (leave) her dog at home.
5. **Marisa** _____ (I / probably / have) a problem if I _____ (not leave) my dog at home.
6. **Gavin** Why _____ (Marisa / have) a problem if she _____ (take) her dog to the concert?
   Mario Her dog hates rock music!

Take another look!

Circle the correct answers.

1. The word *if* can go _____ of a sentence.
   a. only at the beginning
   b. only in the middle
   c. at the beginning or in the middle
2. In which sentence is the speaker sure she will go out?
   a. I'll go out if it stops raining.
   b. I'll go out when it stops raining.
   c. I might go out after the rain stops.

Go to page 128 for the Theme Project.

Lesson 13: Teens online

1 Language focus

A How do teens use the Internet? Read the information. Then listen and practice.

- Finding information for schoolwork is a popular online activity.
- Teens also like chatting with their friends online.
- Downloading music is popular with teens, too.
- E-mailing is popular, but most teens enjoy chatting online more than e-mailing.
- Playing games and watching videos are popular online activities for some teens.
- Shopping online isn't very popular with teens. Maybe that's because they enjoy hanging out at the mall.

The number of teens who use the Internet for:

Finding information for schoolwork	57%
Chatting with friends online	34%
Downloading music	33%
E-mailing	32%
Playing games	19%
Watching videos	14%
Shopping	6%

Source: CBSNews.com

B Study the chart. Complete the sentences with the correct forms of the verb phrases in the box. Then listen and check.

Gerunds as subjects	Gerunds as objects
Finding information for schoolwork is the most popular online activity.	Teens also like **chatting** with their friends online.
Downloading music is popular with teens, too.	Do teens enjoy **shopping** online? Yes, they do. / No, they don't.

☐ do crossword puzzles ☐ find information ☑ play chess
☐ download music ☐ get sports scores ☐ shop for clothes

1. _Playing chess_ online is my favorite thing to do.
2. I like _____ in English online. I learn new words.
3. Ellie buys all of her T-shirts online. She enjoys _____ online.
4. _____ online is easy. I can buy many songs.
5. _____ online is faster than going to the library.
6. I like _____ for all my favorite teams online.

UNIT 4 People

2 Word power

A Create gerund phrases by matching the words in the box to the correct gerunds.

☐ bed late ☐ classes ☐ soccer
☐ board games ☐ crossword puzzles ☐ the movies
☑ chores ☐ homework online ☐ the piano

doing _chores_ _____ _____
going to _____ _____ _____
playing _____ _____ _____

B Complete the sentences about your likes and dislikes with gerund phrases. Use ideas from Part A or your own ideas.

1. _____ on the weekend is fun.
2. I really enjoy _____ with my family.
3. I don't like _____ in the morning.
4. _____ is my favorite activity after school.
5. I don't like _____ on the weekend.

3 Speaking

A Complete the questions about your interests. Then answer them with your own information.

What are your interests? Do you . . . ?	You	Your classmate
1. like listening to _____ (a type of) music	_____	_____
2. enjoy going to _____ (a place)	_____	_____
3. like watching _____ (a TV show)	_____	_____
4. enjoy playing _____ (a sport)	_____	_____
5. like getting up at _____ (a time)	_____	_____
6. enjoy studying _____ (a school subject)	_____	_____

B Ask a classmate the questions. Write his or her responses in the chart. For *No* answers, give the correct information.

Do you like listening to jazz?

No, I don't. I like listening to rock music.

C Now share two interesting things about your classmate with the class.

Mario likes getting up at 6 a.m. He doesn't like playing basketball.

Lesson 14: Personality types

1 Word power

A Complete the sentences about each person with the words in the box. Then listen and practice.

☐ bad-tempered ☑ forgetful ☐ independent ☐ outgoing ☐ trustworthy
☐ creative ☐ hardworking ☐ organized ☐ thoughtful

1. Abby doesn't remember things sometimes.
   She's forgetful.

2. Sara often gets angry.
   _____

3. Jimmy isn't shy and is very friendly.
   _____

4. Cindy doesn't want any help doing things.
   _____

5. Ken keeps things in order.
   _____

6. Andy is very honest.
   _____

7. Lynn makes beautiful things.
   _____

8. Colin always does nice things for people.
   _____

9. Dora and Estelle always do many chores at home.
   _____

B Complete the sentences with the names of classmates.

1. _____ is creative.
2. _____ is hardworking.
3. _____ is outgoing.
4. _____ is thoughtful.

46 Unit 4

2 Language focus

A Trisha and Patsy talk about their personalities. Listen and practice.

too	
I'm thoughtful.	I am, too.
I make friends easily.	I do, too.
either	
I'm not bad-tempered.	I'm not, either.
I don't always remember things.	I don't, either.

Trisha Hey, let's do this survey on personalities.
Patsy OK. Sounds like fun.
Trisha So, about me. I don't always remember things.
Patsy I don't, either. I forgot my lunch today!
Trisha Another one. I'm not bad-tempered.
Patsy I'm not, either. I hardly ever get angry.
Trisha Oh, I like this one. I make friends easily.
Patsy I do, too. I guess I'm outgoing.
Trisha Here's another. I'm thoughtful. Well, I hope I am.
Patsy I am, too. I like to help people.
Trisha Oh, boy! This one. I'm not at all organized.
Patsy I'm afraid I'm not, either. My room is always a mess!
Trisha Hey, we're a lot alike! I guess that's why we're best friends.

B Jack and Roy are talking. Roy agrees with Jack. Complete the conversations with *too* or *either*. Then listen and check.

1. **Jack** I'm outgoing.
   Roy _I am, too._

2. **Jack** I'm not creative.
   Roy _____

3. **Jack** I don't remember things.
   Roy _____

4. **Jack** I keep things in order.
   Roy _____

3 Speaking

Complete the sentences. Add one sentence of your own. Then compare your answers with a classmate.

1. I _____ (am / am not) organized.
2. I _____ (enjoy / don't enjoy) doing things alone.
3. I _____ (have / don't have) a good imagination.
4. I _____ (do / don't do) my homework every night.
5. _____

> I'm organized.   I am, too.   I'm not organized.   I'm not, either.

People 47

Lessons 13 & 14 Mini-review

1 Language check

A Mark is a new student in the class. He and Liam are going to work together on a science project. Complete the conversations with *I am, too; I do, too; I'm not, either;* or *I don't, either.*

B Complete the sentences with the correct form of *do*, *go*, or *play*.

1. Some students enjoy ___playing___ chess. It's a popular activity at some schools.
2. _____ crossword puzzles helps you learn new words.
3. Kim loves _____ the piano. It really helps her relax.
4. _____ to bed late isn't good for you. You'll probably be tired the next day.
5. My brother doesn't like _____ chores on the weekend.
6. _____ to the movies is a fun weekend activity. You can see your favorite movie stars.
7. _____ board games with your family can be fun.
8. Some teens enjoy _____ to concerts with their friends.

C Complete the questions with the correct forms of the verbs. Then answer the questions with your information.

1. (watch TV) Do you like ___watching TV___?
   ___Yes, I do.___
2. (hang out at the mall) Do your friends like _____?
   _____
3. (talk on the phone) Do you enjoy _____ with your friends?
   _____
4. (do homework online) Do your friends like _____?
   _____
5. (play computer games) Does your best friend enjoy _____?
   _____
6. (read books) Does your mother enjoy _____ for fun?
   _____

2 Listening

Teens talk about themselves. Listen and write the correct responses. Use *I am, too; I do, too; I'm not, either;* or *I don't, either.*

1. ___I do, too.___
2. _____
3. _____
4. _____
5. _____
6. _____

Go to page 117 for the Game.

Lesson 15: Unusual people

1 Language focus

A Read about these unusual people. Complete the sentences with the simple present or the simple past. Listen and check. Then practice.

> **who clauses**
>
> **Simple present**
> I have a cousin. She collects spiders.
> I have a cousin **who collects spiders**.
>
> **Simple past**
> I know a woman. She lived and worked in an ice hotel.
> I know a woman **who lived and worked in an ice hotel**.

Do you know anyone who has an **unusual talent**? A **strange habit**? An **interesting collection**? Write and tell us. The best story wins a prize.

1. I have a cousin who _collects_ (collect) spiders. She has more than 40 spiders in her collection.
—Sarah

2. I know a woman who lived and _____ (work) in an ice hotel in Sweden. She slept on a bed made of ice.
—Connor

3. I had a friend who _____ (be) a one-man band. He traveled all over the world.
—Elizabeth

4. I know a man who _____ (ride) a horse to work every day. He lives on my street.
—Kelley

5. I have a friend who _____ (teach) in a circus school last year. He's a lion tamer.
—Michael

6. I know a five-year-old boy who _____ (talk) to animals. He says he understands dogs better than people!
—Antonio

B Who do you think should win the prize for the best story? Tell the class.

> I think Connor should win. The story about the ice hotel is cool!

C Combine the two sentences to make one sentence. Then listen and check.

1. I know a boy. He plays four instruments.
   <u>I know a boy who plays four instruments.</u>

2. I met a woman. She was an Olympic champion.
   _____

3. I had a friend. She collected butterflies.
   _____

4. I sent an e-mail to a man. He is 102 years old.
   _____

D Write three sentences about an interesting person you know.

1. _____
2. _____
3. _____

2 Listening

Teens talk about unusual people. Who are they talking about? Listen and number the pictures.

3 Speaking

Read the questions. Check (✓) Yes or No. Then tell the class about two people you know.

Do you know a person who . . . ?	Yes	No
1. has an unusual job	☐	☐
2. is very good at something	☐	☐
3. lived in a foreign country	☐	☐
4. had an interesting experience last year	☐	☐
5. visited an interesting place recently	☐	☐

I know a woman who has an unusual job. She's a cartoon artist. She's my mother.

People 51

Lesson 16 — Who's that girl?

1 Language focus

A Will and Pedro are talking at a party.
Who are they talking about? Listen and practice.

Will Hey, that's Mary. She's the new student, isn't she?
Pedro Yes, she is. And who's that girl with her? You know her, don't you?
Will Yes, I do. That's Sarah Dixon. She's Australian.
Pedro They both have boyfriends, don't they?
Will No, they don't. Sarah has a boyfriend, but I don't think Mary does.
Pedro Who are those guys over there? They're friends, aren't they?
Will Yes, they are. One is Pablo, Sarah's boyfriend.
Pedro Oh, right. He lives in Colombia, doesn't he?
Will Yes, he does.
Pedro And the other one? Who's he?
Will That's Tom Crowe.
Pedro You're in his class, aren't you?
Will Yes, I am. Oh, now I remember. Tom is Mary's boyfriend.
Pedro So, they *do* both have boyfriends. Too bad! Mary is cute!

B Study the chart. Complete the tag questions, and write responses for each question. Then listen and check.

Tag questions and answers with *be*	Tag questions and answers with the simple present
She's the new student, **isn't she**? Yes, she is. / No, she isn't.	He lives in Colombia, **doesn't he**? Yes, he does. / No, he doesn't.
You're in his class, **aren't you**? Yes, I am. / No, I'm not.	You know her, **don't you**? Yes, I do. / No, I don't.
They're friends, **aren't they**? Yes, they are. / No, they aren't.	They have boyfriends, **don't they**? Yes, they do. / No, they don't.

1. You're 18, _aren't you_ ? _No, I'm not._ OR _Yes, I am._
2. Your teachers are hardworking, _____ ? _____
3. Tokyo is in Japan, _____ ? _____
4. You're a student, _____ ? _____
5. You speak Spanish, _____ ? _____
6. You have a brother or a sister, _____ ? _____

52 Unit 4

2 Pronunciation — Intonation in tag questions

A Listen. Notice the rising intonation in these tag questions. Then listen again and practice.

She's from Colombia, isn't she? ↗

He lives in the U.S., doesn't he? ↗

You're Brazilian, aren't you? ↗

We don't have homework, do we? ↗

B Now practice the tag questions in Exercise 1B.

3 Word power

Write the words in the correct columns.

- ☐ has a dog
- ☐ is creative
- ☐ is trustworthy
- ☐ makes friends easily
- ☑ has blue eyes
- ☐ is Peruvian
- ☐ likes to take risks
- ☐ speaks Spanish
- ☐ has curly hair
- ☐ is tall
- ☐ lives in the U.S.
- ☐ wears glasses

Appearance	Personality	Other
has blue eyes	_____	_____
_____	_____	_____
_____	_____	_____
_____	_____	_____

4 Speaking

A How much do you know about your classmates? Write their names and tag questions.

Classmates	Questions
Carlos	You walk to school, don't you?
1. _____	_____
2. _____	_____
3. _____	_____
4. _____	_____

B Ask your classmates the questions in Part A. How many guesses did you get right?

Carlos, you walk to school, don't you?

Yes, I do.

Get Connected
UNIT 4

Read

A Read the article quickly. Circle the correct answers.

1. (Oldest or only / Middle) children are usually hardworking.
2. (Middle / Youngest) children like being the boss at work.

The youngest is the most outgoing.

Taking personality quizzes is a popular thing to do and many people take them, don't they? But now people can discover their personalities – not from a quiz, but from their **birth order**. **Researchers** say that the oldest, **middle**, youngest, and only children in a family will all have very different personalities.

The oldest or only child likes doing well in school. These people are usually hardworking and are **leaders**. Over half of the U.S. presidents were **firstborn** children. They're children who get lots of time and attention from their parents, say researchers.

The middle child is very creative and thoughtful. These children keep **peace** in a family, say researchers. So they're good with words and are friendly and honest. These people enjoy working in creative careers in the arts or in sales.

The youngest child is the most outgoing. These are the children who like going to parties and are not at all shy. And at work, these people are usually the ones who like being the **boss**.

So, what do you think? Are your birth order and personality connected? Only you can decide. But it's really interesting, isn't it?

> **Go** to page 123 for the Vocabulary Practice.

B Read the article slowly. Check your answers in Part A.

C Are these statements true or false? Write *True* or *False*. Then correct the false statements.

1. People ~~don't like~~ *enjoy* finding out about their personalities. *False.*
2. Birth order and personality aren't connected. _____
3. Parents usually give the most attention to their youngest child. _____
4. The middle child in a family likes to keep the peace. _____
5. The youngest child in a family enjoys socializing / going out. _____

54   Unit 4

I'm the only boy!

A 🎧 **May and Phillip talk about their birth order. Listen and answer the questions.**

1. Is May angry about her sister getting a cell phone? _Yes, she is._
2. Is May the youngest child in her family? _____
3. Does Phillip's sister think life is easier for her than Phillip? _____
4. Does Phillip have friends who study hard? _____
5. Is Phillip an only child? _____

B **What do you think? Write *I agree, I disagree,* or *I'm not sure.* Give reasons.**

1. Youngest children have an easy life. _____
2. Getting a lot of attention from your parents is good. _____
3. Being an only child is great. _____
4. Birth order and personality are connected. _____

Your turn

A Answer the questions about your birth order.

1. Are you an only, oldest, middle, or youngest child? _____
2. What are some of your personality traits? Do they match traits of your birth order?
   _____
3. What are some good things and bad things about your birth order?
   _____
4. Which is the best: being a youngest, middle, oldest, or only chid? Why?
   _____

B Write a paragraph about your birth order. Use the answers in Part A to help you.

```
I'm the _____ child in my family . . .
```

People 55

Unit 4 Review

Language chart review

Gerunds as subjects	Gerunds as objects
Going online is fun.	My friends and I love **going** online.

Tag questions and answers with *be*	Tag questions and answers with the simple present
You're in my science class, **aren't you**? 　Yes, I am. / No, I'm not. He's Mexican, **isn't he**? 　Yes, he is. / No, he isn't. They're cousins, **aren't they**? 　Yes, they are. / No, they aren't.	You wear glasses, **don't you**? 　Yes, I do. / No, I don't. She studies a lot, **doesn't she**? 　Yes, she does. / No, she doesn't. They live near you, **don't they**? 　Yes, they do. / No, they don't.

A Complete the questions for a survey.

1. He plays on the basketball team, <u>doesn't he</u>?
   It's enjoyable, <u>isn't it</u>?

2. You hang out with friends a lot, _____?
   That's fun, _____?

3. She has a job in the school office, _____?
   It's hard work, _____?

4. You do crossword puzzles, _____?
   They're interesting, _____?

5. He does homework on Saturdays, _____?
   It's awful, _____?

B Look again at the sentences in Part A. Combine the two sentences to make a question. Use a gerund phrase as the subject. Then answer the questions with your own information.

1. Q: <u>Playing on the basketball team is enjoyable, isn't it?</u>　A: <u>Yes, it is.</u>
2. Q: _____　A: _____
3. Q: _____　A: _____
4. Q: _____　A: _____
5. Q: _____　A: _____

Language chart review

too		either	
I'm hungry.	I am, too.	I'm not tired.	I'm not, either.
I **read** magazines.	I **do**, too.	I **don't play** video games.	I **don't**, either.

who clauses	
Simple present	**Simple past**
I have a friend. She loves studying French.	I read about a man. He collected cars.
I have a friend **who loves studying French**.	I read about a man **who collected cars**.

C Look at the chart. Then complete the conversations.

	A	B
Age	15	15
Organized	no	no
Hardworking	yes	yes
Likes pizza	no	no

1. **A** I'm 15.
   B *I am, too.*
2. **A** I'm not organized.
   B _____
3. **A** I'm hardworking.
   B _____
4. **A** I don't like pizza.
   B _____

D Combine the two sentences to make one sentence with a *who* clause.

1. Renata Costa is a Brazilian soccer player. She played in her first World Cup game at 17.

   Renata Costa is a Brazilian soccer player who played in her first World Cup game at 17.

2. Al Gore was a U.S. vice president. He won the Nobel Peace Prize.

   _____

3. Vitor Faverani is a Brazilian basketball player. He's 6 feet 11 inches tall.

   _____

4. Sally Ride was an astronaut. She was the first American woman in space.

   _____

5. Paul McCartney is a British singer. He was a member of the Beatles.

   _____

Take another look!

Read the sentences. Write *T* (true) or *F* (false).

1. Gerunds always end with *-ing*. _____
2. In tag questions, the verb (*aren't, doesn't,* etc.) comes after the pronoun (*you, he,* etc.). _____

Go to page 129 for the Theme Project.

People 57

Lesson 17 For fun

1 Language focus

A What have these students done for fun during the week? Listen and practice.

I've been really busy this week. I've read three books, I've hung out with friends at the skate park, and I've played video games at the video arcade. I haven't done all of my homework, though. I haven't had time! My parents aren't very happy about that. —Will

We've been really busy this week, too. We've gone out almost every night. We've seen a couple of movies, and we've gone to a basketball game at school. We've also rented three videos so far. We haven't watched any TV this week, though. We haven't had any time!
—Diana and Jessica

B Study the chart. Complete the sentences with the present perfect. Then listen and check.

Present perfect with *I* and *We*
The present perfect is formed with the verb *have* + the past participle.
I've been busy this week. **We've gone out** every night.
I haven't done all of my homework. **We haven't watched** any TV.
Regular past participles: play → play**ed**   rent → rent**ed**   watch → watch**ed**
Irregular past participles: be → **been**   go → **gone**   read → **read**
do → **done**   hang → **hung**   see → **seen**
eat → **eaten**   have → **had**

1. Juan: <u>I haven't done</u> (not do) many interesting things this week. Let's see . . . _____ (play) video games, and _____ (go) to the mall with my father. But _____ (not see) any movies, and _____ (not eat out) at any restaurants. _____ (do) a lot of homework, though!

2. Carla and Pedro: _____ (be) very busy this week. _____ (have) two karate classes, and _____ (go) canoeing. _____ (watch) a tennis match, too. But _____ (not watch) soccer on TV, and _____ (not read) any comic books!

2 Word power

A Make verb phrases by adding *do*, *make*, or *play*.

make a cake	_____ exercises	_____ homework
_____ chores	_____ friends	_____ money
_____ the piano	_____ a game	_____ plans

B Write three things you have done and three things you have not done this week. Use ideas in Part A or your own ideas. Then tell a classmate.

I've made a cake.
I haven't done chores.

1. _____
2. _____
3. _____
4. _____
5. _____
6. _____

> I've made a cake, . . .

3 Speaking

A What have you done this week? Look at the Fun-O-Meter. Check (✓) the sentence that best describes you. Then find a classmate for each level of fun. Write your classmates' names in the chart.

What have you done this week?	You	Classmates
I've done lots of fun activities this week.	☐	_____
I've done three or four fun activities this week.	☐	_____
I've done one or two fun activities this week.	☐	_____
I haven't done any fun activities this week.	☐	_____

Really a Lot of Fun
A Lot of Fun
A Little Fun
Not Fun at All

Fun-O-Meter

> I've done three or four fun activities this week. How about you, Sally?

> I've done lots of fun activities this week.

B Now tell the class about someone like you.

> Jane and I have done three fun activities this week. We've been very busy.

Entertainment 59

Lesson 18: Young entertainers

1 Word power

Which five of these activities would you most like to do or have happen? Circle the activities. Then listen and practice.

1. become a big star

2. entertain a live audience

3. give interviews

4. have a hit TV show

5. make a movie

6. record a song

7. sign autographs

8. support a charity

9. win a great award

2 Language focus

A Read about these young entertainers. Then listen and practice.

Angelina Jordan
Singer
Angelina Jordan is only 9, but she's become a big star. Millions of people have seen Angelina perform on YouTube. She's performed on TV, and she's sung in many events around the world. During her trips, she's met many famous people. Angelina has won *Norway's Got Talent award*, and that was incredible! Some people in Norway haven't heard her sing, but they might someday!

Amandla Stenberg
Model, actor, and voice actor
Millions of people have seen Amandla perform. She's acted as Rue in *The Hunger Games* movie series. She's also been on TV and people have heard her voice in *Rio 2*. Amandla hasn't won an Emmy for her acting, but she'd like to win an Emmy someday.

Akai Osei and Theo Stevenson
Actors and dancers
Friends Akai Osei and Theo Stevenson have become big stars. Akai Osei has made several movies and he's performed on TV. Theo has been in movies, too. He hasn't sung in a movie, but he'll probably do it someday. Akai and Theo have danced together in *All Stars*.

B Study the chart. Write the past participles from Part A.

Present perfect with *he*, *she*, and *they*	
She's **become** a big star.	She hasn't **won** an Emmy.
He's **performed** on TV.	He hasn't **sung** in a movie.
They've **danced** together in All Stars.	They haven't **heard** her sing.

1. (he / see) _he's seen_
2. (they / act) _____
3. (she / sing) _____
4. (they / be) _____
5. (she / win) _____
6. (he / become) _____
7. (they / make) _____
8. (she / perform) _____
9. (they / record) _____
10. (she / meet) _____
11. (he / give) _____
12. (he / hear) _____

C Complete the sentences with the present perfect. Then listen and check.

1. She _'s appeared_ (appear) in fashion magazines.
2. They _____ (not record) any hit songs.
3. She _____ (compete) in the Olympic Games twice.
4. He _____ (not act) in any plays on Broadway in New York City.
5. They _____ (win) a lot of tennis matches this year.
6. They _____ (sell) millions of their CDs.
7. He _____ (not make) any movies this year.

3 Listening

A radio host interviews a fan about Haley Joel and Emily Osment. Which star is the information about? Listen and check (✓) the correct boxes.

Who . . . ?	Theo	Akai
1. was nine years old in 2007	✓	☐
2. made a movie in 2010	☐	☐
3. has lived on a farm	☐	☐
4. has worked more in TV	☐	☐
5. hasn't sung in movies	☐	☐
6. is going to record his own music	☐	☐

Entertainment 61

Lessons 17 & 18

1 Language check

A Complete Ramiro's biography of Kany Garcia. Use the present perfect.

Kany Garcia

- Kany Garcia was born in 1982 in Puerto Rico.
- Her family is very musical. Her brother plays the cello in the Puerto Rican Symphony Orchestra. She _'s studied_ (study) classical cello and the guitar. But she really loves singing, too.
- Kany _____ (write) many songs. People call her music intelligent and beautiful. For her, the words of a song are very important.
- She _____ (record) an album with Sony Records. She _____ (win) a Gold Album. It _____ (sell) more than 100,000 copies.
- Kany _____ (receive) four Latin Grammy nominations, but she _____ (not win) a Grammy.
- She _____ (not record) an album in English.
- Kany _____ (support) a special charity for children in Puerto Rico.

B Complete the e-mail message. Use the present perfect.

Hi, James!

I _'ve been_ (be) really busy this week. I _____ (make) a Web site about Kany Garcia. Do you know her? She's a young singer from Puerto Rico. My sister and I _____ (become) big fans of hers. I _____ (learn) a lot about her and her music from different places on the Internet. I _____ also _____ (buy) her first album. She _____ (give) a big concert in Puerto Rico, but she _____ (not perform) around here. Anyway, I hope I can share information about her with other kids on this Web site. I _____ (not have) much experience making Web sites! Please check it out and let me know what you think.

Ramiro

62   Unit 5

C Ken, Emily, and Jamie have been busy this week. Look at the chart. Then complete the sentences about the things they have done (✓) and the things they haven't done (✗).

	Ken	Emily	Jamie
Do chores	✗	✗	✗
Make plans for Saturday	✗	✓	✗
Play the piano	✗	✓	✓
Hang out with friends	✓	✗	✗
Watch TV	✓	✗	✓
Eat out	✓	✓	✓

1. They _haven't done chores_____.
2. Emily _____.
3. Ken and Jamie _____.
4. Emily and Jamie _____.
5. Ken _____.
6. Ken _____.
7. Emily and Jamie _____.
8. Ken and Jamie _____.
9. Emily _____.
10. They _____.

2 Listening

A A student reporter is interviewing Natalia and Manuel for the school newspaper. Are the sentences true or false? Listen and write *T* (true) or *F* (false).

1. Natalia has learned a lot from her ~~brother~~. _F_ (mother)
2. She has climbed Mount Baldy three times. ____
3. She hasn't visited the Andes. ____
4. Manuel and Miguel have performed on TV. ____
5. They haven't sold many CDs. ____
6. Radio stations have played their CD. ____

B Listen again and correct the false statements in Part A.

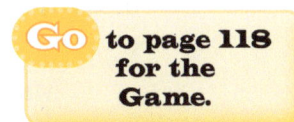

Entertainment 63

Lesson 19: Are you a fan?

1 Language focus

A Carla and Pedro are buying tickets for a concert. Listen and practice.

> **Present perfect Yes/No questions with ever**
> **Have you ever gone** to a concert?
> Yes, I have. / No, I haven't.
> **Has she ever met** Kylie Minogue?
> Yes, she has. / No, she hasn't.

Pedro Hi, Carla. Are you in line for the Kylie Minogue concert?
Carla Yes, I am. I'm so excited!
Pedro Have you ever gone to one of her concerts?
Carla Yes, I have. I've been to ten of her concerts!
Pedro Wow! This will be my first Kylie concert. Have you ever gotten her autograph?
Carla No, I haven't. Have you?
Pedro No, I haven't, but my friend Lily has. She's been to every Kylie concert here.
Carla Has she ever met Kylie?
Pedro Yes, she has. She met her backstage at a concert last year. She always gets invited backstage.
Carla Then let's go with her to the concert. I can't wait to meet Kylie!

B Complete the conversations. Then listen and check.

1. **Sam** ___Have___ you _ever gotten_ (get) a sports star's autograph?
   Maggie Yes, I _____ .

2. **Pia** _____ Matt _____ (go) to a rock concert?
   Beth Yes, he _____ .

3. **Kim** _____ your best friend _____ (win) a radio contest?
   Kayla No, she _____ .

4. **Tom** _____ you _____ (write) a fan letter?
   Bill No, I _____ .

5. **Kate** _____ your sister _____ (met) a famous singer?
   Ellen Yes, she _____ .

6. **Jack** _____ your brother _____ (have) a girlfriend?
   Matt Yes, he _____ . He's had two girlfriends.

64 Unit 5

2 Listening

Diane and Julio are fans of Jordin Sparks. Who has done these things, Diane or Julio? Listen and write *D* (Diane) or *J* (Julio).

Who has . . . ?	
1. gotten Jordin's autograph	*D*
2. met Jordin	___
3. written a fan letter to Jordin	___
4. received a postcard from Jordin	___
5. bought a Jordin Sparks poster	___
6. gotten a ticket to one of her concerts	___

3 Pronunciation   Stress in *Have you ever*

A Listen. Notice the stress in *Have you ever* questions. Then listen again and practice.

Have you **ever** met a **rock** star?   Have you **ever** won a **ticket**?

Have you **ever** climbed a **mountain**?   Have you **ever** eaten **snails**?

B Now practice the questions in Exercise 1B.

4 Speaking

A Write five *Have you ever* questions. Then ask a classmate (Classmate A) the questions, and check (✓) Yes or No.

	Classmate A	
	Yes	No
Have you ever met a sports star?	☐	☐
1. _____	☐	☐
2. _____	☐	☐
3. _____	☐	☐
4. _____	☐	☐
5. _____	☐	☐

B Ask another classmate (Classmate B) the questions in Part A. Classmate B guesses Classmate A's answers. How many did he or she guess right?

You Has Jake ever met a sports star?
Classmate B Yes, he has.
You Right. Has Jake ever studied French?
Classmate B Yes, he has.
You Wrong. He hasn't studied French.

Entertainment   **65**

Lesson 20 Pop culture trivia

1 Language focus

A Are you good at pop culture trivia? Find out. Check (✓) the correct answers. Listen and check. Then practice.

> **How long has / How long have . . . ?**
> **since** and **for**
>
> **How long has** Harrison Ford had a star on the Walk of Fame?
>   He's had a star **since May 2003**.
>   **Since May 2003.**
> **How long has** Johnny Depp acted in movies?
>   He's acted in movies **for about 25 years**.
>   **For about 25 years.**

1. How long has Harrison Ford had a star on the Walk of Fame?
   ☑ Since May 2003.
   ☐ Since May 1993.

2. How long has Johnny Depp acted in movies?
   ☐ For about 13 years.
   ☐ For about 30 years.

3. How long has Hollywood been the center of the movie industry?
   ☐ Since the 1920s.
   ☐ Since the 1950s.

4. How long has the Statue of Liberty been a popular tourist attraction?
   ☐ For about 100 years.
   ☐ For about 130 years.

5. How long have people celebrated New Year's Eve in Times Square?
   ☐ For over 100 years.
   ☐ For over 50 years.

6. How long has the modern Internet been around?
   ☐ Since 2001.
   ☐ Since 1995.

B Write two interesting trivia questions about your life. Ask a classmate the questions. Can your classmate answer correctly?

1.
2.

You How long have I had a pet rabbit?
Classmate You've had a pet rabbit for three years.
You Right.

66 Unit 5

C Complete the questions and answers. Then listen and check.

1. the company Paramount Pictures / be / in Hollywood

    Q: <u>How long has the company Paramount Pictures been in Hollywood?</u>

    A: <u>It's been in Hollywood since</u> 1913. OR <u>Since</u> 1913.

2. Jamie Foxx / have / a star on the Hollywood Walk of Fame

    Q: _____

    A: _____ September 14, 2007.

3. people / have / color TVs

    Q: _____

    A: _____ over 50 years.

4. rock music / be / popular

    Q: _____

    A: _____ a long time.

5. actors / receive / Oscars at the Academy Awards

    Q: _____

    A: _____ 1927.

2 Listening

Jessica, Diana, and Carla appear on a TV game show about pop culture trivia. Listen and check (✓) the correct answers.

1. Broadway Tony Awards
   - ☐ since 1927
   - ☐ since 1947

2. MGM Studios
   - ☐ since 1924
   - ☐ for 100 years

3. CDs
   - ☐ since the 1970s
   - ☐ since the 1980s

4. Grauman's Chinese Theatre
   - ☐ for about 50 years
   - ☐ for about 75 years

3 Speaking

A Imagine you will interview a famous actor. Complete questions 1 and 2. Write question 3.

1. <u>How long have you been</u> (be) an actor?
2. _____ (live) in Hollywood?
3. _____

B Now role-play the interview with a classmate. Make up the answers.

Entertainment 67

Get Connected
UNIT 5

Read

A Read the article quickly. Check (✓) the main idea of the article.

☐ 1. Reality shows are only for very talented singers.

☐ 2. Reality show performers always become very successful.

☐ 3. You need luck and talent to win on a reality show.

How to Be Rich and Famous

Have you ever watched a **reality show** on TV? Of course you have! They're some of the most popular shows on TV. People have watched reality shows for many years, but they became really popular several years ago with shows like *American Idol*. Millions of **viewers** all over the world have seen this show, and thousands of people have performed on the show. They want to win **recording contracts** and become famous singers. Some of the show's winners have sold millions of CDs, and they now have successful singing **careers**.

So, what kind of reality show do you want to perform on? Have you ever told jokes to people, and have they laughed? Then maybe you can try a reality show for **comedians**. Are you a good dancer? Yes? Then try a reality show for dancers.

Research says that one in seven young people would like to go on a reality show and become famous. So, **go ahead** – **audition** for a show. And if you do . . . good luck!

Go to page 124 for the Vocabulary Practice.

B Read the article slowly. Check your answer in Part A.

C Answer the questions.

1. How long have reality shows been popular? *They've been popular for many years.*

2. Have a lot of people performed on *American Idol*?

3. What do the people on *American Idol* want to win?

4. What has happened to some of the show's winners?

5. What other kinds of reality shows are there?

You should go on that show.

A Ricardo and Jill talk about reality shows. Listen and answer the questions.

1. Who taught Jill everything she knows about cooking?
   <u>Her grandmother taught her everything she knows about cooking.</u>
2. Has Jill ever seen the reality show *Top Chef*?
   _____
3. What do the winners on *Top Chef* win?
   _____
4. What places have the teams on *Survivor* been to?
   _____
5. What kind of show would Ricardo like to go on?
   _____

B What do you think? Answer the questions. Give reasons.

1. Why do you think reality shows are so popular? _____
2. Have you ever watched any reality shows? Which ones? _____
3. Have you or your friends ever auditioned for a reality show? _____
4. Do you think reality shows are a good way to start a career? _____

Your turn

A Imagine you have just won a reality show contest. Answer the questions.

1. What kind of reality show is it? _____
2. Were you surprised about winning? _____
3. Was it exciting to win? Why? _____
4. What did you win? _____
5. Has your life changed? How? _____

B Write a paragraph about winning a reality show contest. Use the answers in Part A to help you.

I've just won . . .

Entertainment 69

Unit 5 Review

Language chart review

Present perfect statements	
Affirmative	**Negative**
I've seen two movies this week.	**I haven't eaten** in a restaurant.
He's had a lot of fun this week.	**He hasn't been** home much.
They've made three new friends.	**They haven't done** their homework.

A Look at Rosie's date book. It's Thursday night. What has she done this week? What hasn't she done? Complete the sentences about Rosie and her friends and family.

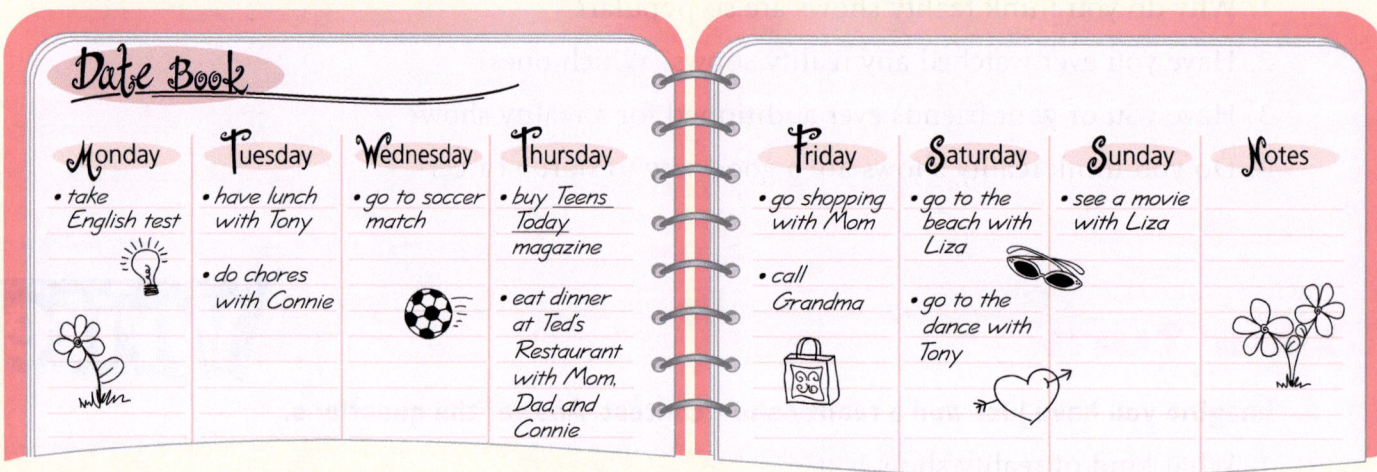

1. Rosie _has taken_ an English test.
2. She and her friend Liza _haven't gone_ to the beach.
3. Rosie and her family _____ at a restaurant.
4. She _____ to the soccer match.
5. She _____ *Teens Today* magazine.
6. Rosie _____ her grandmother.
7. She _____ a movie.
8. Rosie and her little sister Connie _____ chores at home.
9. She and her friend Tony _____ lunch together.

B Now it's Saturday night. What has Rosie done since Friday? What hasn't she done? Complete the sentences with the present perfect.

I've had (have) an awesome time so far! _____ (do) a lot of interesting things. _____ (go) shopping with Mom. _____ (go) to the beach with Liza. Tony and I went to the dance tonight. It was great! _____ (not see) a movie with Liza. I'll do that tomorrow. Uh-oh. I _____ (not do) any homework!

Language chart review

Present perfect Yes/No questions with *ever*	How long has / How long have ... ? *since* and *for*

Have you ever lived in an apartment?
  Yes, I have. / No, I haven't.
Has he ever gone to Africa?
  Yes, he has. / No, he hasn't.
	How long have you had your cell phone?
	  I**'ve had it since Friday**. / **Since Friday**.
	How long has Kimmy lived in London?
	  She**'s lived in London for about five years**.
	  For about five years.

C Read about the new students at Kennedy Junior High. Write questions. Then complete the answers.

Kaya Morita

Kaya and her family moved here six months ago. She started at Kennedy on Monday. Her favorite memory: She traveled to Australia last year. Her wish for the future: She would love to write a book someday.

Rob and Dave Borelli

Rob and Dave came to Kennedy two weeks ago. Their favorite memory: They met Gustavo Kuerten. Their wish for the future: They want to win a tennis tournament someday.

1. **Q:** (visit Australia) <u>Has Kaya ever visited Australia?</u>
   A: _____ . Kaya and her family visited Australia last year.

2. **Q:** (be at Kennedy) _____
   A: _____ . She just started school.

3. **Q:** (write a book) _____
   A: _____ , but she'd like to write a book someday.

4. **Q:** (win a tennis tournament) _____
   A: _____ , but they want to.

5. **Q:** (meet a sports star) _____
   A: _____ . They met Rafael Nadal at a tennis match.

Take another look!

Read the sentences. Then check (✓) all the sentences that are true for Sue.

Sue says, "I've lived in Mexico City since June."

a. ☐ Sue lives in Mexico City now.
b. ☐ Sue moved to Mexico City a few years ago.
c. ☐ Sue used to live in another place.
d. ☐ Sue hasn't lived in Mexico City for a very long time.

Go to page 130 for the Theme Project.

Lesson 21

Taking risks

1 Word power

A Look at the pictures. Then listen and practice.

1. dye my hair

2. explore a cave

3. ride a motorcycle

4. go out without permission

5. go rock climbing

6. go skydiving

7. sing karaoke

8. start a rock band

9. try new foods

B Complete the sentences with the correct phrases from Part A.

1. He's going to a mountain with big rocks. He might _go rock climbing_ .
2. I love the color blue. I'd like to _____ blue.
3. She loves rock music and plays the guitar. Someday, she's going to _____ .
4. They love to eat. They always like to _____ .
5. I'd like to _____ . I like to go fast. Do you think my parents will give me permission?
6. He's not shy, and he loves to sing. He'll _____ .
7. They love to fly. Maybe someday they'll _____ .
8. My friend's parents say he can't go out on Saturday, but he's going to _____ . That's bad.
9. He likes discovering new places. He might _____ .

UNIT 6 Experiences

72

2 Language focus

A Juan and Will are talking about risks. Listen and practice.

Juan Hey, Will. Have you ever gone rock climbing?
Will No, I haven't. I've never gone rock climbing. And I don't want to try it.
Juan So, I guess you're not going to go on the school rock-climbing trip?
Will No. But I'm going to go on the skydiving trip. I'm excited!
Juan You're kidding, right? Have you ever gone skydiving?
Will No, never. But there's always a first time. Do you want to come?
Juan No, thanks. I've never jumped from a plane, and I never want to try.

> **Present perfect with *never***
>
> I've **never** gone skydiving.
> I've **never** jumped from a plane.
>
> **Have** you **ever gone** rock climbing?
>   No, I **haven't**. I've **never** gone rock climbing.
>   No, **never**.
>
> Note: *Never* isn't used in questions with the present perfect.

B Juan asks Will more questions about risks he has taken. Will has not done any of these things. Listen and write his answers.

1. Have you ever ridden on a motorcycle? <u>No, never.</u>
2. Have you ever sung karaoke? <u>No, I haven't. I've never sung karaoke.</u>
3. Have you ever had a pet snake? _____
4. Have you ever taken a trip alone? _____
5. Have you ever dyed your hair? _____
6. Have you ever eaten worms? _____
7. Have you ever gone out without permission? _____
8. Have you ever started a rock band? _____

3 Speaking

Work with a classmate. Take turns asking and answering the questions in Exercise 2B.

> Have you ever ridden on a motorcycle?

> No, never. Have you ever sung karaoke?

> No, I haven't. I've never sung karaoke. Have you ever . . .

Experiences

Lesson 22: What we've done

1 Language focus

A What have Ally, Matt, and Kristopher done in the last year? Listen and practice.

Ally
I love to travel. I think it's fun. I've been to a lot of places, and I've seen many interesting things since last summer. Last month, I went to London with my parents. We stayed there for two weeks. We did a city tour and saw Big Ben. It's so tall! I was really sad to leave London.

Matt
I started a band called The Green Tomatoes a year ago. We play rock music, and I'm the lead singer. We've practiced in a friend's garage for six months, but we have to find another place to practice soon. Since January, we've played more than 20 shows. It's been fun so far!

Kristopher
I've won two marathons so far this year. In February, I won the school marathon. Last month, I won the city marathon. I've also won three shorter races since the city marathon. I love running. I never want to stop!

B Study the chart. Then read Kristopher's text in Part A again. Write his first four sentences in the correct columns in the chart. Then listen and check.

Simple past		Present perfect	
•———•———• Now	Time phrases: last month, a year ago, in February, for two weeks	⌒ Now	Time phrases: since last summer, so far, for six months
Last month, I **went** to London with my parents. I **started** a band **a year ago**. We **stayed** there **for two weeks**.		I**'ve seen** many interesting things **since last summer**. We**'ve practiced for six months**. It**'s been** fun **so far**.	

74 Unit 6

C Complete the texts about these students. Use the simple past or the present perfect. Then listen and check.

1. Last year, Cam ____spent____ (spend) six months in Canada on an exchange program. He _____ (stay) with a Canadian family. He _____ (come) back in December. Since then, he _____ (e-mail) his Canadian parents every day. Marc, his Canadian brother, is now staying with Cam and his family. He _____ (be) there for five months.

2. We _____ (have) three family reunions since 2000, and I _____ (meet) more than 100 relatives so far at these parties. Last summer, we _____ (have) a big picnic near the ocean. I _____ (go) scuba diving with my cousins. Two days ago, my mother _____ (tell) me that we are going to have another reunion this summer!

2 Listening

Julie and Ray talk about experiences they have had. Are the sentences true or false? Listen and check (✓) True or False.

	True	False
1. Julie saw a skydiving movie when she was eight.	☐	☑
2. She went skydiving four months ago.	☐	☐
3. She's gone skydiving more than 20 times.	☐	☐
4. Ray has collected postcards for about ten years.	☐	☐
5. He got his first postcard from his grandfather.	☐	☐
6. He bought 100 postcards last week.	☐	☐

3 Speaking

A Complete the sentences with your own experiences. Try to think of interesting things. Then tell a classmate about them.

I _____ since last _____.   I _____ ago.
I _____ so far this _____.   I _____ last _____.

> I've read three books in English since last month. I went to Disney World last year.

B Tell the class about one of your classmate's experiences.

> Jack went to South Africa last summer.

Experiences 75

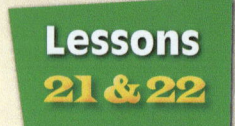

Lessons 21 & 22 Mini-review

1 Language check

A Complete the conversation. Use the present perfect and *ever* or *never*.

Brenda Do you like to try new foods?
Bobby   Yes, I do.
Brenda _Have_ you _ever tried_ (try) Thai food?
Bobby   Yes, I love Thai food.
Brenda _____ you _____ (eat) at the Thai restaurant on Main Street?
Bobby   No, I haven't. I _____ (eat) there. Have you?
Brenda No, never. Let's go sometime.
Bobby   Good idea. _____ you _____ (be) to a Peruvian restaurant?
Brenda No. I _____ (be) to one. Is there one in our town?
Bobby   Yes, there is. There's one next to the library. Come on! Let's go!

B Look at Amanda's calendar. Today is September 14th, and she's at the library. Complete the sentences. Use the simple past or the present perfect, and *for*, *since*, *ago*, or *so far*.

SEPTEMBER

Sunday	Monday	Tuesday	Wednesday	Thursday	Friday	Saturday
1 Move to Florida	**2** First day of school. Buy notebooks.	**3** Swimming practice 3:00 p.m.	**4** First piano lesson after school	**5** Swimming practice 3:00 p.m.	**6**	**7** Movie with Sue
8	**9**	**10** Swimming practice 3:00 p.m.	**11** Out to dinner with family	**12** Swimming practice 3:00 p.m.	**13**	**14** Library 10:00 a.m. Study all day. **TODAY**

1. _She's lived_ (live) in Florida _since_ September 1st.
2. She _____ (be) in school _____ two weeks.
3. She _____ (buy) some notebooks 12 days _____ .
4. She _____ (be) to four swimming practices _____ .
5. She _____ (go) out to dinner with her family three days _____ .
6. She _____ (be) at the library _____ 10:00 a.m. this morning.
7. She _____ (see) one movie _____ .
8. She _____ (study) piano _____ last week.

76 Unit 6

C Complete the e-mail messages and replies. Use the simple past or the present perfect. Then match each message to the correct reply.

1

Hi there, Carl!
I _had_ (have) a wonderful vacation last month! My family and I _____ (go) on an ecological tour of a rain forest. We _____ (stay) in a hotel high up in the trees of the rain forest. It _____ (be) awesome. _____ you _____ (ever be) to a rain forest?
Carrie

2

Hi, Alberto!
_____ you _____ (ever go) white-water rafting? I _____ (try) it a month ago, and I _____ (hate) it. It _____ (be) so scary! I never want to do it again.
Michael

3

Hey, Maria!
What a boring weekend I had! I _____ (buy) a new computer game on Saturday, but my father _____ (use) the computer all weekend! I _____ (not play) it at all since I bought it! I have only five minutes to write my e-mails now, and I _____ (use) three minutes already. I have to hurry. Bye!
Laura

☐ Oh, come on. It's not that bad. My friends and I _____ (go) several times. It _____ (be) really exciting.

☐ That's too bad. You need your own computer. I _____ (have) mine since last summer, and I use it all the time.

☐ No. I _____ (never be) to one. I'd love to go! Tell me more!

2 Listening

Students ask some questions. Listen and check (✓) the correct responses.

1. ☑ Yes, I have. It was great.
   ☐ Yes, I did. It was great.

2. ☐ Are you kidding? No, I haven't.
   ☐ Are you kidding? No, I didn't.

3. ☐ No, never. I never have.
   ☐ No, I didn't.

4. ☐ For a long time.
   ☐ Last month.

5. ☐ A month ago.
   ☐ Since last spring.

6. ☐ Since last year.
   ☐ A year ago.

Go to page 119 for the Game.

Lesson 23: Amazing teens

1 Language focus

A Read about these amazing teens. Then listen and practice.

> **has already / hasn't ... yet**
> **Affirmative statements with already**
> Mo'ne **has already** taken a place in the Hall of Fame.
> Arvind **has already** won a big money prize.
> **Negative statements with not ... yet**
> Mo'ne **hasn't** learned every trick **yet**.
> Arvind **hasn't** finished high school **yet**.

Mo'ne Davis is 14, and she's a baseball star. Everyone who sees Mo'ne play says she's amazing. She can throw the ball very fast. She started playing baseball when she was five years old. She's already appeared on the cover of *Sports Illustrated* magazine and taken a place in the National Baseball Hall of Fame. Mo'ne hasn't learned every baseball trick yet. There are always new ones to learn. Mo'ne also plays soccer and basketball and is an excellent student. She's still in middle school, but she's already played basketball on the high school team at Springside Chestnut Hill Academy, in Philadelphia.

Mo'ne Davis

Fifteen-year-old Arvind Mahankali is a spelling whiz. He was the winner of the 2013 Scripps National Spelling Bee Contest – a spelling contest for teenagers in the United States. The spelling bee is the largest spelling contest in the United States. The contest appears nationally on television. Arvind wants to be a physicist. He has always liked physics. He hasn't finished high school yet, but he has already won a $30,000 prize.

Arvind Mahankali

B Complete the sentences about John and Elizabeth with the correct verbs from Part A. Use *already* or *not ... yet*. Then listen and check.

1. (a place in the National Baseball Hall of Fame) Mo'ne <u>has already taken a place in the National baseball hall of Fame</u>.
2. (every trick) Mo'ne _____.
3. (high school team) Mo'ne _____.
4. (a spelling contest) Arvind _____.
5. (high school) Arvind _____.
6. (a $30,000 prize) Arvind _____.

2 Listening

American gymnast Norah Flatley is another amazing teen. What has she already done? What hasn't she done yet? Listen and check (✓) the correct boxes.

Shawn has . . .	Already	Not yet
1. studied with a famous Chinese gymnast.	✓	☐
2. won many gymnastics competitions.	☐	☐
3. won a lot of money.	☐	☐
4. been on television shows.	☐	☐
5. finished high school.	☐	☐

3 Word power

A Write the verb phrases in the box in the correct columns.

✓ decide on a career	☐ get a job	☐ study a foreign language
☐ get a college degree	☐ go to a rock concert	☐ turn 16 years old
✓ get a driver's license	☐ have a boyfriend or a girlfriend	☐ vacation in a foreign country

Personal	School and career
get a driver's license	decide on a career
_____	_____
_____	_____

B Write sentences about yourself. Use phrases from Part A or your own ideas.

I haven't decided on a career yet.

1. _____
2. _____
3. _____
4. _____

4 Speaking

Compare your information from Exercise 3B with a classmate. Then tell another classmate.

Helen I haven't gotten a driver's license yet.
Ana I've already decided on a career.

> Helen hasn't gotten a driver's license yet.

> Ana has already decided on a career.

Experiences 79

Lesson 24 — In the spotlight

1 Language focus

A Kira and Leo are studying for a test on the book *The Adventures of Tom Sawyer.* **Listen and practice.**

Kira Let's review for our English reading test on the first half of *The Adventures of Tom Sawyer*.

Leo OK, Kira. Let's see how much we know. Bret Harte wrote *The Adventures of Tom Sawyer*, didn't he?

Kira No, he didn't. Mark Twain wrote it. He was a famous American writer.

Leo Oh, right. He wrote a lot of books, didn't he?

Kira Yes, he did.

Leo OK. Let's see . . . So far in the book, Tom and his brother Sid have lived with their Aunt Polly for a long time, haven't they?

Kira Yes, they have. Next question: Tom and Sid have always been very different, haven't they?

Leo Yes, they have. Sid has been a good boy, but Tom has often behaved badly.

Kira But Tom has always liked school, hasn't he?

Leo No, he hasn't. He's never liked school.

Kira Oh, yes, I forgot. Anyway, so far Tom has really liked adventures, hasn't he?

Leo Yes, he has. Wait! I have one more question for you. We'll get a good grade on the test, won't we?

Kira Well . . .

B Study the chart. Then complete the sentences with tag questions.

Tag questions with the simple past	Tag questions with the present perfect

He **wrote** a lot of books, **didn't** he?
  Yes, he **did**.
Bret Harte **wrote** *The Adventures of Tom Sawyer*, **didn't** he?
  No, he **didn't**.
	They**'ve lived** with her for a long time, **haven't** they?
	  Yes, they **have**.
	Tom **has** always **liked** school, **hasn't** he?
	  No, he **hasn't**.

1. You spoke English yesterday, _____ ?
2. Your friends visited you at home last week, _____ ?
3. You have always lived in the same house, _____ ?
4. You were at school yesterday, _____ ?

80   Unit 6

C Read about Julia Roberts and her niece Emma Roberts. Complete the tag questions and answer them. Then listen and check.

> Julia Roberts was born in 1967. She's an actor and has appeared in more than 30 movies and in one Broadway play. Julia's niece, Emma Roberts, has been in several TV shows and she's starred in the movie *Nancy Drew*. Emma's father (Julia's brother), Eric, is also an actor. They've all been very successful.

1. Julia Roberts was born in 1967, <u>wasn't she</u>? <u>Yes, she was.</u>
2. She's made more than 30 movies, _____ ? _____
3. Her niece Emma became a singer, _____ ? _____
4. Emma starred in the movie *Runaway Bride*, _____ ? _____
5. Julia, Eric, and Emma have been successful, _____ ? _____

2 Listening

A Kira and Leo take a trivia quiz about Denzel Washington. Are these sentences true or false? Listen and check (✓) T (true) or F (false).

	T	F
1. Denzel Washington was born in California.	☐	✓
2. He studied drama in college.	☐	☐
3. His first big part was in a musical.	☐	☐
4. He's won two Oscars.	☐	☐
5. He and his wife have four children.	☐	☐
6. He's acted in about 50 movies.	☐	☐

B How many of your answers are correct? Compare with a classmate.

> Denzel Washington was born in California, wasn't he?

> No, he wasn't.

3 Pronunciation Intonation in tag questions

A Listen. Notice the intonation in tag questions. Then listen again and practice.

He studied computer science in college, didn't he?

They were married about 25 years ago, weren't they?

He's acted in about 40 movies, hasn't he?

He was on *General Hospital*, wasn't he?

B Now practice the tag questions in Exercise 1D.

Experiences 81

Get Connected
UNIT 6

Read

A Read the article quickly. Check (✓) the phrases you find.

☐ ate a spider ☐ lived in a glass box ☐ stayed under water
☐ jumped out of an airplane ☐ read people's thoughts ☐ stood on a 30-meter pole

Incredible!

If you ask most people around the world, "Have you ever heard of David Blaine?" the answer will probably be, "No, never." But ask New Yorkers the same question, and they will probably say, "Yes, we have."

David first became popular for his TV show. Several years ago, on his first show, he walked around the streets of New York and entertained people with amazing tricks. He made money disappear and things appear from nowhere. And he read people's thoughts. Everyone was **amazed**.

But David isn't just an entertainer – he also does **stunts**. Since his first TV show, David has spent 72 hours inside a **block** of ice, he's stayed under water in a huge glass **bowl** for 7 days, he's lived in a glass box for 44 days with no food, and he's stood on a 30-meter **pole** for 35 hours. His audiences have never been disappointed.

He's not 45 yet, but he's already written a book about his life. The title of his book – *Mysterious Stranger* – probably describes him really well. Not everyone knows about David yet, but they will someday.

Go to page 124 for the **Vocabulary Practice.**

B Read the article slowly. Check your answers in Part A.

C Answer the questions.

1. Have most New Yorkers heard of David Blaine? _Yes, they have._
2. How did he first become popular? _____
3. Has he ever stayed under water for a long time? _____
4. Have his audiences ever been disappointed? _____
5. Has he ever written a book? _____

You've gotten good then, haven't you?

A 🔊 **Dimitri and Heidi talk about stunts. Listen and answer the questions.**

1. Has Heidi ever seen motorcycle stunts on TV? _Yes, she has._
2. What does she think about the stunts? _____
3. Has Dimitri ever done any stunts? _____
4. Has he ever had any accidents? _____
5. Has Heidi ever been to the skateboard park? _____

B **What do you think? Answer the questions. Give reasons.**

1. Do you think people should do dangerous stunts on TV?
   _____
2. Do you think being a stunt person is a good career? _____
3. Why do you think people choose to do dangerous hobbies? _____
4. What do you think parents should say if their children want to try a dangerous hobby? _____

Your turn

A **Think about some dangerous hobbies. Answer the questions.**

1. Have you ever tried a dangerous hobby? Why or why not? _____
2. Do you know anyone who has a dangerous hobby? _____
3. How do you feel when people do dangerous hobbies or stunts? _____
4. Would you like to try something dangerous? What? _____
5. What would your family and friends think if you did? _____

B **Write a paragraph about a dangerous hobby. Use the answers in Part A to help you.**

_I_ _tried a dangerous hobby because . . ._

Experiences 83

Unit 6 Review

Language chart review

Present perfect with *never*

He's **never** driven a car.
We've **never** gone rock climbing.

Have they **ever** explored a cave?
Yes, they **have**. / **No**, they **haven't**.
No, never. They've **never** explored a cave.

has already / hasn't . . . yet

Affirmative statements with *already*	Negative statements with *not . . . yet*
I've **already** turned 14.	She **hasn't** decided on a career **yet**.

A Look at the pictures. Then write sentences with *already* or *yet* and the verb phrases in the box.

☐ dye hair purple   ☐ explore a cave   ☑ go skydiving   ☐ start a rock band

1. He's already gone skydiving.
2. _____

3. _____
4. _____

B Look at the chart. Have Alana and Rick ever done these things? Write questions and answers.

Climb a mountain	Eat worms
Alana ✓ Rick ✗	Alana ✗ Rick ✓

1. **Q:** Has Alana ever climbed a mountain?
   A: Yes, she has.
2. **Q:** _____
   A: _____
3. **Q:** _____
   A: _____
4. **Q:** _____
   A: _____

Language chart review

Simple past	Present perfect
I **got** a job **in May**. He **learned** a lot **last year**.	I**'ve met** many interesting people **since May**. **Since last spring**, we**'ve made** a lot of money.

Tag questions with the simple past and present perfect

Simple past	Present perfect
You **called** her yesterday, **didn't** you? Yes, I **did**. / No, I **didn't**.	You**'ve come** to class every day, **haven't** you? Yes, I **have**. / No, I **haven't**.

C Complete the postcards with the simple past or the present perfect.

Dear Carlos,
<u>We've been</u> (we / be) in New York City since last Friday. Our first hotel _____ (be) noisy, so we _____ (move) to a quieter place. Last night, we _____ (eat) at the Hard Rock Cafe, and I _____ (see) Miley Cyrus! I _____ (take) a picture of her with my new camera. She _____ (give) me her autograph!
See you soon,
Connie

Hi, Sonia!
_____ (I / be) in New York for almost a week. We _____ (get) here last Friday. We _____ (hear) the buses and cars all night, so we _____ (move) to a quieter hotel. The weather _____ (be) beautiful. Yesterday we _____ (buy) a new camera. I'll e-mail you some pictures this afternoon.
Connie

Sonia Alvarez
432 Park Street
San Francisco, CA 94105

D Look again at the postcards in Part C. Complete the tag questions. Then write the answers.

1. **Q:** Connie bought a new camera in New York City, <u>didn't she</u> ?
   A: _____

2. **Q:** Their first hotel was noisy, _____ ?
   A: _____

3. **Q:** The weather in New York City has been terrible, _____ ?
   A: _____

4. **Q:** Connie got Natalie's autograph, _____ ?
   A: _____

Take another look!

Are these time phrases used with the simple past (*SP*), with the present perfect (*PP*), or both (*SP & PP*)?

1. so far _____
2. last Saturday _____
3. for a month _____
4. a week ago _____

Go to page 131 for the Theme Project.

Lesson 25

Teen opinions

1 Language focus

A Read these teens' opinions about movies and music. Then listen and practice.

> good / better / the best
> bad / worse / the worst
>
> Action movies are **good**.
> Comedies are **better than** action movies.
> Science-fiction movies are **the best** movies of all.
> I think rap music is **bad**.
> Rock music is **worse than** rap music.
> Pop music is **the worst** music of all.
>
> | Adjective | Comparative | Superlative |
> |---|---|---|
> | good | better | the best |
> | bad | worse | the worst |

I'm a big movie fan, so I like all kinds of movies. Action movies are OK, but I think comedies are better than action movies. They make me laugh. Science-fiction movies are the best movies of all. The stories are always interesting. I've seen all of the *Star Trek* movies three times. They're great! **– Andrea**

I only listen to country music and jazz music. They're the only kinds of music I like. I think rap music is bad. I can't understand the words. And rock music is worse than rap music. It's too loud. But take my advice. Pop music is the worst music of all because it's so boring. **– Bart**

B Complete the sentences with the correct words. Then listen and check your answers.

1. I love history. I think it's <u> the best </u> (the best / the worst) subject at school. It's easy for me.
2. Sports are great. Volleyball is a _____ (good / bad) sport to play with friends, but I think soccer is better than volleyball.
3. I can't stand dramas. The stories are boring. They're _____ (the best / the worst) shows on TV.
4. School uniforms are great. Wearing a uniform is much _____ (better than / worse than) wearing your own clothes to school.
5. I don't like doing the dishes. But I think cleaning my room is _____ (better than / worse than) doing the dishes. I don't like chores.
6. I really like pizza, but the pizza at Rocco's is _____ (bad / good). It tastes awful. It's the worst pizza in my neighborhood.

UNIT 7 Teen Time

86

2 Word power

A Which of these words have positive meanings? Which have negative meanings? Write the words in the correct columns.

☑ awful   ☐ dangerous   ☐ entertaining   ☐ forgetful   ☐ messy   ☐ thrilling
☑ beautiful   ☐ difficult   ☐ excellent   ☐ hardworking   ☐ scary   ☐ trustworthy

Positive		Negative	
beautiful	_____	awful	_____
_____	_____	_____	_____
_____	_____	_____	_____

B Complete these opinions with the best words from Part A.

1. Roller coasters are the best amusement park rides! I'm never afraid on roller coasters. They're not ___scary___ at all.
2. I think skydiving is a bad sport because you can get hurt. It's very _____ .
3. My math test grade is worse than my English test grade. I think math is very _____ .
4. I think Pink is the best singer right now. She's pretty, too. She has a _____ face.
5. Comedies are better than thrillers. They aren't as exciting, but they're more _____ .

3 Speaking

A What's your opinion? Complete the chart with examples of each thing.

	Good	Better	The best
Singers			
Actors			
TV shows			

	Bad	Worse	The worst
Chores			
Movies			

B Share your opinions with the class.

> I think "Singer A" is a good singer. "Singer B" is better than "Singer A." "Singer C" is the best singer.

Lesson 26: Unforgettable moments

1 Language focus

A Read about these teens' unforgettable moments. Complete the texts with the superlative + *ever* and the correct form of the verbs. Listen and check. Then practice.

> **Superlative + ... have ever ...**
> Parasailing is **the scariest** thing I**'ve ever done**.
> It's **the most disgusting** food we**'ve ever eaten**.
> It's **the weirdest** present he**'s ever received**.

1. Parasailing is the scariest thing I've ever done. I never want to do it again.

2. We ate crocodile meat on a safari once. It's the most disgusting food we've ever eaten.

3. My brother's friend gave him a spider for his birthday. It's the weirdest present he's ever received.

4. I got 40 percent on my math test last week. It's _____ (bad) grade I've _____ (get).

5. Beyoncé is _____ (good) singer I've _____ (hear). I went to her concert last year. It was great.

6. Jenny fell during a play. It's _____ (embarrassing) experience she's _____ (have).

B Complete the sentences with your opinions. Then tell the class.

1. _____ is the scariest thing I've ever done.
2. _____ is / are the most disgusting food I've ever eaten.
3. _____ is the weirdest present I've ever received.

> Riding a roller coaster is the scariest thing I've ever done.

C Read the statements and write sentences with the superlative + *ever* and the correct form of the verbs. Then listen and check.

1. I got 100 percent on the test last week.
   (good grade / get) It's the best grade I've ever gotten.

2. My friend Tom got lost in a strange city late at night.
   (scary experience / have) _____

3. My sister bought *Quest*, a new computer game.
   (exciting game / play) _____

4. My brother erased his favorite computer files by mistake.
   (frustrating thing / do) _____

5. Kate studied Japanese last summer.
   (difficult language / study) _____

6. I spent the weekend reading *Silly Stories*.
   (funny book / read) _____

2 Listening

Look at these titles and listen to the stories. What is the best title for each one? Listen and number the titles.

Title	Number
"The Most Interesting Place I've Ever Visited"	_____
"The Worst Car Ride I've Ever Had"	_____
"The Scariest Moment I've Ever Had"	_____
"The Most Embarrassing Experience I've Ever Had"	_____

3 Speaking

Complete the survey for yourself. Then ask a classmate the questions.

What's the . . . ?	You	Your classmate
1. best movie you've ever seen	_____	_____
2. worst book you've ever read	_____	_____
3. most interesting place you've ever visited	_____	_____
4. best vacation you've ever had	_____	_____

What's the best movie you've ever seen?

The Fault in Our Stars is the best movie I've ever seen.

Teen Time 89

Mini-review

1 Language check

A Read the critic's ratings of burger places and online music stores. Then complete the sentences with *better than*, *worse than*, *the best*, or *the worst*.

BURGER PLACES ★★★★

Burger City ★★★★
The burgers here are great. They're big, tasty, and juicy. The french fries are OK. The only problem is the noise. It's always very crowded and very loud.

Burger and Fries ★★★
The burgers are OK, and the french fries are OK. It sometimes gets crowded, and it's a little loud, but you can usually get a table.

Galaxy Burger ★★
The burgers aren't very good at all, but the french fries are delicious. The place usually isn't very crowded, so noise isn't a problem.

ONLINE MUSIC STORES ★★★★

YourTunes#123 ★★★
This Web site has a big music selection, from rock to jazz. You can find and download almost anything you want. The download time is very fast. The only problem is that the prices are the highest online, and there isn't any free music.

BestTunesEver ★★
This Web site sells a variety of popular music, but there are many songs you can't find on the site. Also the download time on this Web site is really slow. But the prices are really low, and you can get some music for free here.

AlwaysClassicTunes ★★★★
This Web site only has classical music and jazz. If that's what you're looking for, you'll find it here. The prices are lower than the prices on YourTunes. This site also offers a lot of information about the music. The other sites don't.

1. The burgers are <u>the best</u> at Burger City.
2. The burgers at Burger City are _____ the burgers at Burger and Fries.
3. The burgers are _____ at Galaxy Burger.
4. The fries at Galaxy Burger are _____ the fries at Burger and Fries.
5. The fries at Galaxy Burger are _____ in town.
6. The noise at Burger City is _____ the noise at Burger and Fries.
7. The music selection at YourTunes#123 is _____ the selection at BestTunesEver.
8. The prices at YourTunes#123 are _____ online.
9. Always ClassicTunes is _____ site for classical music and jazz.
10. The download time at BestTunesEver is _____ the download time at YourTunes#123.

B Katie and Mike are on the quiz show *Do You Know Your Family?* Write answers with the superlative + *ever* and the correct form of the verb.

Host Good evening everyone. Tonight Katie Wilson and her brother Mike are going to answer questions about their family. Katie, has your father ever done anything scary?

Katie Well, he went rock climbing once. I think (scary / did) <u>it's the scariest thing he's ever done</u>.

Host OK. Now, Mike. Has your mother ever had a thrilling experience?

Mike Definitely. She went skydiving last month. I think (thrilling experience / have) _____.

Host OK. Now Katie, you and Mike have twin brothers, Joe and Jim. Do they like funny movies?

Katie They love them. They saw *A Clown's Life* last week. I think (funny movie / see) _____.

Host And Mike. What about Katie? What's something disgusting she has eaten?

Mike Oh, once some kids made her eat a worm. I think (disgusting thing / eat) _____.

Host And a question for you, Katie. Has Mike ever read a bad book?

Katie Oh, yes. He read *How to Be Happy*. I think (bad book / read) _____.

Host One more question. Mike, have your mom and dad visited any beautiful places?

Mike Hmm. They loved the Grand Canyon. I think (beautiful place / visit) _____.

2 Listening

A Listen to the rest of the quiz show from Exercise 1B. Were Mike and Katie's answers correct or incorrect? Check (✓) Correct ($1,000) or Incorrect ($0) for each question.

	Correct ($1,000)	Incorrect ($0)
1.	☐	✓
2.	☐	☐
3.	☐	☐
4.	☐	☐
5.	☐	☐
6.	☐	☐

B How much money did Mike and Katie win? Add together the number of correct answers in Part A. Then write the number below.

Mike and Katie won $ _____ .

Go to page 120 for the Game.

Lesson 27 Are we alike?

1 Language focus

A What do you know about Cole and Dylan Sprouse? Read Elena's Web site about them. Then listen and practice.

Kendall and Kylie Jenner

Welcome to my Jenner sisters Web site. I think these sisters are awesome. They're both models and television personalities. Kylie is as famous as Kendall, but she isn't as old as her. She's two years younger. Anyway, I hope you enjoy my Web site.

Facts about the Jenner sisters

They were both born in Los Angeles, California. Kylie was born on August 10, 1997. Kendal was born on November 3, 1995. Their parents are American. They're both talkative and outgoing. Kendall loves animals. She is four inches taller than Kylie. She's 5 feet, 10 inches tall (179 cm).

▼ And who am I?

My name's Elena, and I'm a fan of Kylie and Kendall Jenner. Am I as famous as them? No, I'm not. I'm also younger than they are. Here's my photo and some more information about me.

▼ Facts about me

I was born on June 11. I'm 5 feet, 4 inches tall (163 cm). I'm funny, but I'm shy. I'm athletic, but I'm not good at tennis. I have one brother, Dario. He was born on June 11. We're twins, too!

B Study the chart. Rewrite the sentences with informal comparisons. Then listen and check.

Formal comparisons: as…as / not as…as	Informal comparisons: as…as / not as…as + object pronoun
Kylie is **as famous as** Kendall. Kylie is **as famous as** she is.	Kylie is **as famous as her**.
I'm **not as famous as** the Jenner sisters. I'm **not as famous as** they are.	I'm **not as famous as them**.
	Object pronouns: *me, you, him, her, it, us, them*

1. Elena isn't as tall as the Jenner sisters. _She isn't as tall as them._
2. Dario is as old as Elena is. _____
3. Elena isn't as famous as Kylie and Kendall are. _____
4. The Jenner sisters aren't as young as Dario is. _____
5. Kendall Jenner isn't as short as I am. _____

92 Unit 7

C Read the information about Kylie Jenner. How are you alike? How are you different? Write sentences using informal comparisons.

> Kylie Jenner was born on August 10, 1997. She's 5 feet, 6 inches tall (168 cm). She likes running and she likes taking pictures. Kylie's favorite school subject is math.

1. (age) _____
2. (height) _____
3. (interests) _____

2 Word power

A Check (✓) the word in each category that does not belong.

1. sports   ☐ athletic   ☐ active   ☐ artistic   ☐ strong
2. school   ☐ lazy   ☐ serious   ☐ smart   ☐ hardworking
3. making friends ☐ outgoing   ☐ bad-tempered ☐ friendly   ☐ funny
4. helping others ☐ thoughtful ☐ trustworthy   ☐ kind   ☐ forgetful

B Complete the sentences with words from Part A and object pronouns.

1. You're better at sports than me. I'm not as _athletic_ as _you_ .
2. My sister draws well. I do, too. I'm as _____ as _____ .
3. My brother is lazier than I am. He's not as _____ as _____ .
4. My father isn't shy when he meets people. I'm not, either. I'm as _____ as _____ .
5. Our neighbors are always telling jokes. No one is as _____ as _____ .

3 Speaking

Compare yourself to people in your life. Tell your classmates. Use the ideas in the chart or your own ideas.

People	Characteristics	Good at
best friend	artistic	computer games
cousins	musical	math
brother or sister	athletic	cooking
neighbors	outgoing	languages
teacher	creative	making friends
your mom or dad	thoughtful	sports

> My friend Mike is athletic. I am, too. I'm as athletic as him.

> My cousins are good at math. I'm not. I'm not as good at math as them.

Lesson 28: I'd rather . . .

1 Language focus

> **would . . . rather for preferences**
> **Would** you **rather** be rich **or** famous?
> **I'd rather** be famous.
> **I'd rather** be rich **than** famous.

A Carla and Will talk about a survey. Who would rather be famous? Listen and practice.

Carla What are you looking at, Will?
Will This survey. It has some interesting questions. Listen to this one. "Would you rather be rich or famous?"
Carla Oh, that's an easy choice. I'd rather be famous. A famous singer, a famous actor, a famous poet . . . I'd love to be famous all over the world!
Will Well, not me. I'd rather be rich than famous. I'd like to have lots of money to buy anything I want!
Carla Really? I don't think money is important.
Will You don't? Then could you lend me $30?
Carla What? $30? Are you kidding?
Will But, Carla, money isn't important . . .

B Write questions and answer them with your own preferences. Then listen and check.

1. **Q:** (listen to rap / to rock music) <u>Would you rather listen to rap or rock music?</u>

   A: <u>I'd rather listen to rap than rock music.</u> OR <u>I'd rather listen to rock music than rap.</u>

2. **Q:** (have a car / a motorcycle) _____

   A: _____

3. **Q:** (swim / run) _____

   A: _____

4. **Q:** (meet an actor / a sports star) _____

   A: _____

5. **Q:** (read a book / a magazine) _____

   A: _____

C Tell your classmates about your preferences.

> I'd rather listen to rap than rock music.

2 Listening

A Diana and Juan answer questions for a TV show. Who would rather do or be these things? Listen and check (✓) the correct names.

Who would rather . . . ?	Diana	Juan
1. go to the beach than the mountains	☐	✓
2. be rich than famous	☐	☐
3. be a singer than an actor	☐	☐
4. have a pet dog than a pet cat	☐	☐

B Write the answers to the questions in Part A.

1. Juan would rather go to the beach than the mountains.
2. _____
3. _____
4. _____

3 Pronunciation   Intonation in questions of choice

A Listen. Notice the intonation in questions where there is a choice. Then listen again and practice.

Would you rather swim or run?   Would you rather be a singer or an actor?

B Practice the questions in Exercise 1B.

4 Speaking

A Work with a classmate. What would your classmate rather do? Ask questions. Use the verb phrases in the box or your own ideas.

do chores / homework
join a theater group / a rock band
eat meat / vegetables
buy music / clothes
play video games / a sport
learn karate / to play a musical instrument

Ricardo, would you rather do chores or homework?

I'd rather do chores.

B Tell the class about your classmate.

Ricardo would rather do chores than homework.

Get Connected
UNIT 7

Read

A Read the Web site quickly. Check (✓) what one teen wrote about a trip.

☐ "It was amazing. It's the most interesting place I've ever been."

☐ "It's one of the greatest experiences I've ever had. It made me a better person."

Amazing Experiences

Would you rather go on a trip next summer or stay at home? That's an easy question for the thousands of teens who have traveled all over the world with AAVE (All About Visiting Earth). They'd rather go on an exciting summer trip with AAVE than stay at home. But AAVE isn't just a travel company. AAVE believes that experiencing a culture is better than only traveling to a country. So, teens who travel with the company do **community work**, study languages, and learn outdoor **wilderness skills**.

Recently, some teens went to China. They walked on the Great Wall, learned about **pandas** at a center for pandas, and worked with **farmers**. They also taught English to children, and they studied Chinese.

On the VETC blog, teens say summers with the company are the best they've ever had. Many teens think that spending time together is as much fun as traveling. One teen who traveled to Africa wrote, "It's one of the greatest experiences I've ever had. It made me a better person."

One thing is certain: After a **memorable** experience like this, these teenagers aren't the same as they were before.

Go to page 125 for the Vocabulary Practice.

B 🔄 Read the Web site slowly. Check your answer in Part A.

C Are these statements true or false? Write *T* (true) or *F* (false). Then correct the false statements.

1. Teens who have traveled with VETC would ~~like to stay home~~. _F_
   rather go on an exciting VETC trip

2. VETC thinks cultural experiences are better than only traveling to a country. _____

3. Teens say VETC trips are the best they've ever had. _____

4. VETC teens think spending time together isn't as much fun as traveling. _____

5. After traveling with VETC, teens are the same as they were before. _____

I'd rather go with you.

A 💿 **Carlos and Luisa talk about an exciting experience. Listen and answer the questions.**

1. Where's Carlos going on his next vacation? _He's going to Peru._
2. What's one of the most interesting places in Peru? _____
3. Is Carlos going to study Spanish there? _____
4. What's the most important part of the trip? _____
5. What would Luisa rather do – go to music camp or go on the trip with Carlos? _____

B **What do you think? Answer the questions. Give reasons.**

1. Do you think it's important for young people to travel?
   _____
2. Would you rather travel in your own country or travel to other countries? _____
3. Do you think it's important to learn other languages? _____
4. Do you think it's good to try new things? _____

Your turn

A **Think of an exciting experience you've had (taking a trip, trying an activity). Answer the questions.**

1. What did you do? When? _____
2. How did you feel? _____
3. Was it the best experience you've ever had? _____
4. Would you like to do it again? _____
5. What other experiences would you like to try? _____

B **Write a paragraph about an exciting experience. Use the answers in Part A to help you.**

_About _____ ago, I ..._

Teen Time 97

Unit 7 Review

Language chart review

good / better / the best	bad / worse / the worst
Nellie's is a **good** restaurant.	The Hawks are a **bad** baseball team.
Burger Barn is **better than** Nellie's.	The Eagles are **worse than** the Hawks.
Tom's Diner is **the best** restaurant in town.	The Bobcats are **the worst** team in the city.

Superlative + ... have ever ...

He's **the messiest** person she's **ever met**.
Those are **the most beautiful** flowers I've **ever seen**.

A Complete the conversations. Use the correct forms of the words in parentheses.

1. **A** How did you do on the history exam?
   B I got 63 percent. It's <u>the worst grade I've ever gotten</u> (bad grade / get)! How about you?
   A My grade is even worse than yours. I got 55 percent.

2. **A** What a great game!
   B This is _____ (good game / see)!
   A I'm not sure about that. You were at last week's game, weren't you? That game was _____ (good) than this one. It was really exciting.
   B You might be right.

3. **A** Do you want to go out to eat?
   B Sure. Let's go to Dino's. They have _____ (good) pizza in town.
   A I can't go to Dino's. The last time I was there, I dropped my tray in the middle of the restaurant. It was _____ _____ (embarrassing thing / do)!

4. **A** I think this movie is _____ (bad) than *Action Man*, the movie we saw last week.
   B I agree. It's _____ (bad movie / see).
   A It wasn't even _____ (scary) than *Action Man*.
   B I hope the movie we'll see next week will be _____ (good) than this one.

98 Unit 7

Language chart review

Formal comparisons: *as ... as / not as ... as*	Informal comparisons: *as ... as / not as ... as* + object pronoun
Ines is **as tall as** Tom. Ines is **as tall as** he is. I'm **not as tall as** Ines and Tom. I'm **not as tall as** they are.	She's **as tall as him**. I'm **not as tall as them**. Object pronouns: *me, you, him, her, it, us, them*

would ... rather for preferences
Would you **rather** have a cat **or** a dog?
   I'd rather have a cat.
   I'd rather have a cat **than** a dog.

B Complete the comparisons of Sally and Jack with *as ... as* or *not as ... as*.

1. Jack is lazy. Sally isn't. Sally is <u>n't as lazy as Jack</u>.
2. Jack is smart, and Sally is, too. Jack is _____.
3. Sally is tall, and Jack is, too. Sally is _____.

Sally   Jack

C Complete the sentences about Sally and Jack with object pronouns.

1. Sally and Jack are very strong, but Jack isn't as strong as <u>her</u>.
2. My friends and I are athletic. Sally and Jack aren't as athletic as _____.
3. Jack loves meeting new people. But Sally isn't as friendly as _____.
4. Sally and Jack are really tall. I'm not as tall as _____.

D Write questions for numbers 1 and 2. Then answer number 3 with your own information.

1. **Q:** <u>Would you rather read a book or watch TV?</u>
   A: I'd rather read a book than watch TV.
2. **Q:** _____
   A: I'd rather do a homestay in Canada than in England.
3. **Q:** Would you rather eat at home tonight or go to a restaurant?
   A: _____

Take another look!

Circle the correct answers.
1. Which sentence means the same as "I'm not as hardworking as him"?
   a. I work harder than him.   b. He works harder than me.   c. He works as hard as me.

2. Would you rather travel or stay home?
   a. I'd rather go to school.   b. I'll stay home.   c. I'd rather stay home than travel.

Go to page 132 for the Theme Project.

Teen Time

Lesson 29: Our dreams

1 Language focus

If clauses with could ... would

If I could live in any country in the world, I'd live in Italy.

If Jack could talk to a famous person, he'd talk to Bill Gates.

I'd = I would; he'd = he would

A Trish and her classmates were asked about their dreams. Here are their responses. Complete the texts. Listen and check. Then practice.

Check out our dreams!

Do you think they'll come true?
What's your dream?

1. If I _could live_ (live) in any country in the world, _I'd live_ in Italy. It looks beautiful, and I love Italian food.

2. If Jack _____ (talk) to a famous person, _____ to Bill Gates. He's one of the richest people in the world, and he's very smart.

3. If Jenny _____ (buy) any house in the world, _____ the White House. It's the coolest house she's ever seen.

4. If Hilary _____ (wear) any clothes to school, _____ a pink T-shirt, a pink miniskirt, and pink shoes. She loves pink!

5. If he _____ (be) good at any sport, _____ good at basketball. He'd like to play for the Los Angeles Lakers someday.

6. If they _____ (go) on a trip anyplace in the world, _____ to Africa. They want to go on a safari and see wild animals.

B Write sentences about your dreams. Use the ideas in the box or your own ideas. Then tell a classmate.

| be good at any sport | look like any person | visit anyplace in the world |
| live in any city in the world | talk to any famous person | wear any clothes to school |

If I could live in any city in the world, I'd live in Miami.

1. _____
2. _____
3. _____
4. _____
5. _____
6. _____

If I could live in any city in the world, I'd live in Miami.

2 Pronunciation Pauses

A Listen. Notice the pause in *If* clauses. Then listen again and practice.

If I could live anyplace in the world, I'd live in Paris.

If she could talk to a famous person, she'd talk to Pink.

B Practice your sentences from Exercise 1B.

3 Listening

A Some students talk about their dreams. Listen and match the students to their dreams.

1. Carl ____   a. marry a member of a royal family
2. Rita ____   b. be a professional athlete
3. Liz ____   c. win an event at the Olympic Games
4. Mark ____   d. fly fighter planes

B Listen again. Check (✓) why they have those dreams.

1. Carl ☐ He'd love to travel.   ☐ He'd love to play basketball sometimes.
2. Rita ☐ She loves to travel.   ☐ She loves exciting situations.
3. Liz   ☐ She likes princes.   ☐ She likes people who help others.
4. Mark ☐ He loves horses.   ☐ He has his own horse.

Dreams and Reality

Lesson 30

What would you do?

1 Word power

A Match each verb or verb phrase to its meaning. Then listen and practice.

1. eavesdrop _h_
2. cheat on a test ____
3. break a promise ____
4. gossip ____
5. jaywalk ____
6. lie ____
7. litter ____
8. trespass ____

a. cross the street in the middle of the block
b. say things that are not true
c. enter a private place without permission
d. talk about other people's lives
e. leave paper or garbage around carelessly
f. copy someone's answers
g. not do something you said you'd do
h. listen in secret to someone's conversation

B What are these people doing? Label the pictures.

1. _He's breaking a promise._

2. _____

3. _____

4. _____

5. _____

6. _____

7. _____

8. _____

C Which of these things do you think is the worst behavior? Tell your classmates.

> I think cheating on a test is the worst behavior.

2 Language focus

Unreal conditional with *if* clauses

What **would** you **do if** you **found** $20?
If I **found** $20, **I'd take** it to the teacher.
I'd keep it.

I'd = I would

A What game did Pedro play today?
Listen and practice.

Pedro We played a game today called "What would you do if . . . ?" It made us think about doing the right thing. Did you play the game, too?

Carla No, we didn't. But it sounds interesting. Do you remember any of the questions?

Pedro Yeah. What would you do if you found $20 at school?

Carla I'd keep it, because $20 isn't a lot of money. I mean, it's not the same as finding $1,000! So, what would *you* do if you found $20?

Pedro If I found $20, I'd take it to the teacher. It's not my money, so it doesn't matter how much it is.

Carla You're right. I'd take it to the teacher, too, I guess. What would you do if you saw a person littering?

Pedro I'd ask the person to throw the garbage in the trash can. What would you do?

Carla If I saw a person littering, I'd pick up the garbage and throw it in the trash can.

B Match the two parts of each sentence. Then listen and check.

1. If I found a lot of money on the street, _d_
2. If I saw a classmate cheating on a test, ____
3. If my sister lied to our parents, ____
4. If I heard my friends gossiping about me, ____
5. If I saw my brother jaywalking, ____
6. If my brother was eavesdropping, ____

a. I'd tell them about it.
b. I'd ask them not to talk about me.
c. I'd tell him to cross at the corner.
d. I'd take it to the police.
e. I'd ask him to stop listening.
f. I'd tell him or her to stop copying.

C Write sentences. Choose two *If* clauses from Part B, and complete them with your own information. Then read your sentences to a classmate.

1. _____
2. _____

3 Speaking

Talk with two classmates. Look at the situations in Exercise 2B.
What would you do in each situation?

Maya What would you do if you found a lot of money on the street, Mike?

Mike If I found a lot of money, I'd take it to the police. How about you, Carly?

Carly I'd take it to the police, too. What would you do if . . . ?

Lessons 29 & 30 Mini-review

1 Language check

A Choose the correct words to complete the conversation.

Todd If you ___could___ (could / would) visit any country in the world, where _____ (do / would) you go?

Paula Hmm. If I _____ (could / would) visit any country, I think _____ (I'll / I'd) go to Kenya.

Todd What would you do there?

Paula If I _____ (went / go) to Kenya, _____ (I'm / I'd) go on a safari and see lions in the wild.

Todd Yeah, that would be cool.

Paula What about you? What country would you visit?

Todd If I _____ (have / had) enough time, I'd _____ (visited / visit) Mongolia.

Paula Mongolia! Why?

Todd I saw a documentary about Mongolia on TV. It was beautiful, and the people were fascinating. If I _____ (travel / traveled) to Mongolia, _____ (I'd / I) ride a horse. I'd love that.

B Number the sentences in the correct order.

____ If he gave me his autograph, I'd show it to all of my friends.

____ If I went backstage after the concert, I'd meet Justin Timberlake.

_1_ If I could go to any concert, I'd go to a Justin Timberlake concert.

____ If I met Justin Timberlake, I'd ask him for his autograph.

____ If I went to one of Justin Timberlake's concerts, I'd go backstage after the concert.

104 Unit 8

C Complete the sentences with the clauses in the box.

☐ I'd be a lion
☐ I'd be a movie star
☐ I'd buy an expensive car
☐ I'd study chess
☑ If I could change my appearance
☐ If I could change my personality
☐ If I had a fight with my best friend
☐ If I needed help with my schoolwork

What would you do if ...?

1. _If I could change my appearance_, I'd be taller.
2. If I could have any job, _____.
3. If I could learn any new game, _____.
4. _____, I'd try to be friends again.
5. _____, I'd be more outgoing.
6. If I could be any animal, _____.
7. If I had a lot of money, _____.
8. _____, I'd ask my older sister.

D Write sentences. Use the four *If* clauses from Part C, and add your own information.

1. _____
2. _____
3. _____
4. _____

2 Listening

Chrissa talks about her life and her future dreams. Listen to the questions and check (✓) Yes or No.

	Yes	No		Yes	No
1.	☐	☑	4.	☐	☐
2.	☐	☐	5.	☐	☐
3.	☐	☐	6.	☐	☐

Go to page 121 for the Game.

Dreams and Reality

Lesson 31 — What I'm going to be

1 Word power

A What do these people do? Complete the sentences with the verb phrases. Use the correct forms of the verbs. Then listen and practice.

- ☐ create programs
- ☑ fly planes
- ☐ help sick animals
- ☐ make discoveries
- ☐ make furniture
- ☐ report on events and people
- ☐ solve mysteries
- ☐ travel in outer space
- ☐ write stories

1. A pilot _flies planes_ .
2. An author _____ _____ .
3. An astronaut _____ _____ .

4. A carpenter _____ _____ .
5. A detective _____ _____ .
6. A scientist _____ _____ .

 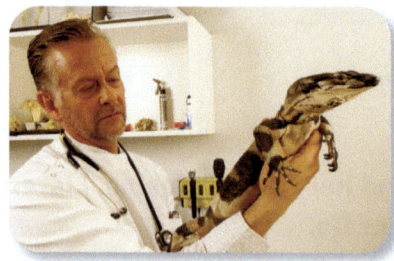 

7. A journalist _____ _____ .
8. A veterinarian _____ _____ .
9. A computer programmer _____ _____ .

B Ask a classmate three questions about what people do. Your classmate names the jobs.

Who reports on events and people? — A journalist.

2 Language focus

A Look at the school yearbook. What does everyone want to be? Why do they want to have that job? Listen and practice.

Lisa Lennox
1. Lisa is going to be a veterinarian to help sick animals.

Dennis Hodge
2. "I want to be a journalist to report on events and people."

Adam and Max Kaufman
3. Adam and Max want to be astronauts to travel in outer space.

Ryoko Ikuta
4. "I want to be a detective to solve mysteries."

B Study the chart. Write sentences with infinitives. For numbers 1–3, use *going to*. For numbers 4 and 5, use *want to*. Then listen and check.

> **Infinitives to give a reason**
>
> I'm going to be a veterinarian. I want to help sick animals.
> I'm going to be a veterinarian **to help** sick animals.
>
> He wants to be a journalist. He wants to report on events and people.
> He wants to be a journalist **to report** on events and people.

1. (Emma / carpenter) *Emma is going to be a carpenter to make furniture.*
2. (Nick and Sue / pilots) _____
3. (Jenny / author) _____
4. (Paul / astronaut) _____
5. (Kim and Kelly / scientists) _____

3 Speaking

A Complete the job survey for yourself. Then ask a classmate the questions.

Do you like to . . . ?	You Yes	You No	Your classmate Yes	Your classmate No		You Yes	You No	Your classmate Yes	Your classmate No
meet people	☐	☐	☐	☐	take risks	☐	☐	☐	☐
spend time on your own	☐	☐	☐	☐	have fun	☐	☐	☐	☐
make or create things	☐	☐	☐	☐	help others	☐	☐	☐	☐
travel	☐	☐	☐	☐	write a lot	☐	☐	☐	☐

B What do you think your classmate would probably like to be one day? Why? Choose a job from Exercise 1A, or use your own ideas. Then tell the class.

> Mario would probably like to be a pilot to travel, to have fun, and to meet people.

Dreams and Reality

Lesson 32 The past year

1 Language focus

A Juan is interviewing Keiko for the school magazine. Has Keiko had a good year or a bad year? Listen and practice.

Juan So, did you do anything really crazy or special last year?
Keiko Well, I didn't do anything crazy, but I did do something really special. I entered a poetry competition, and I won a prize.
Juan Great! What about this year? Have you been anywhere interesting or unusual?
Keiko Oh, I went somewhere fascinating – Antarctica.
Juan Wow! I'm sure that was an incredible trip.
Keiko Yeah! It was awesome!
Juan And have you met anyone special recently?
Keiko Oh, yes. I met someone really special a few weeks ago – a cute guy.
Juan Really? Where did you meet him?
Keiko Well, we met at a party. Then we started going out together, . . . and then he met my sister. He's going out with her now!

B Study the chart. Complete the conversations with indefinite pronouns. Then listen and check.

Indefinite pronouns		
Questions	**Negative statements**	**Affirmative statements**
Did you do **anything** special?	I didn't do **anything** special.	I did **something** really special.
Is there **anywhere** interesting to visit near the school?	I haven't been **anywhere** interesting.	I went **somewhere** fascinating.
Have you met **anyone** special recently?	I haven't met **anyone** special.	I met **someone** really special.

1. **Sam** Is there _anywhere_ interesting to visit near the school?
   Jill Well, maybe. The planetarium. But I don't know _____ about it.
2. **Sam** Have you met _____ interesting recently?
   Jill Yes. I met _____ at a party the other day. He's very funny.
3. **Sam** Is there _____ special you'd like to do this year?
   Jill Oh, yes. I'd like to go _____ fun. Maybe Disney World.
4. **Sam** I just read _____ about the Bahamas. Have you ever been there?
   Jill No. I've never been _____ outside the U.S.

108   Unit 8

2 Listening

A Lucia, Greg, and Megan talk about their experiences this past year. Who is talking? Listen and write the correct name below each picture.

_____   _____   _____

B Listen again and check (✓) the correct name or names.

	Lucia	Greg	Megan
Who has done something special this year?	☐	☐	☐
Who has been somewhere amazing this year?	☐	☐	☐
Who hasn't met anyone special this year?	☐	☐	☐

3 Speaking

A Ask a classmate about things he or she has done in the past year. Use the words in the box or your own ideas.

- do something interesting
- meet someone special
- learn something useful
- go somewhere exciting
- try something new to eat
- read something interesting

> João, have you done anything interesting this year?

> Yes, I have. In June, I learned how to ride a horse. In August, I went . . .

B Tell the class what you found out about your classmate.

> João has done something interesting this year. In June, he learned how to ride a horse. In August, he went somewhere exciting on vacation. He went to Fortaleza. He tried something new to eat. He tried the local food there, crabs. He loved them.

Dreams and Reality 109

Get Connected
UNIT 8

Read

A Read the article quickly. Circle the words you find.

ambassador	cancer	community	donate	foundation
billion	cities	cure	education	skills

If you could do something for the world . . .

What would *you* do if you were rich and famous? Would you stay at home or would you travel? Would you do anything special? Well, some **celebrities** do many special things, and they help millions of people.

Bill Gates, one of the richest people in the world, and his wife, created the Bill and Melinda Gates **Foundation**. It's the largest foundation in the world, and it has $31 **billion** to spend on health and **education** in poor countries.

Angelina Jolie and Brad Pitt, the famous actors, give a lot of money to charity. They sold pictures of their twin babies to a magazine for $14 million! But they gave all the money to charity. And in her **role** as an **ambassador** for the United Nations, Angelina visits the world's poorest countries. She wants everyone to know about problems there.

Elton John, who has played over 3,000 concerts in over 75 countries, is one of the world's greatest singers. He has seen many of his friends die from **AIDS**, so he created the Elton John AIDS Foundation. It has raised over $125 million to support programs on prevention and to help people living with AIDS around the world.

But you don't have to be rich and famous to help. Everyone can do something. If you could do something for the world, what would you do?

Go to page 125 for the Vocabulary Practice.

B Read the article slowly. Check your answers in Part A.

C Are these statements true or false? Write *True* or *False*. Then correct the false statements.

1. Bill and Melinda Gates created their foundation to help people in poor countries.
   True.

2. Brad Pitt and Angelina Jolie sold pictures of their house.
   _____

3. Angelina visits many places to talk about problems in the world.
   _____

4. Elton John donates money to education.
   _____

5. You can only help people if you're rich and famous.
   _____

If I had a million dollars...

A Laurie and Scott talk about being rich. Listen and answer the questions.

1. Why can't Scott get something nice for his mother? *He doesn't have enough money.*
2. Why doesn't Laurie get a part-time job? _____
3. What would Scott do for his parents if he had a million dollars? _____
4. Would he buy anything for himself? _____
5. Does Laurie need a lot of money to have fun? _____

B What do you think? Answer the questions. Give reasons.

1. Do you think it's a good idea for students to work part-time? _____
2. Do you think parents should give a lot of money to their children? _____
3. Do you think it's important to give money to charity? _____
4. Do you agree that you don't need money to have fun? _____

Your turn

A Imagine you have one million dollars. What would you do? Answer the questions.

1. How would you feel if you won a million dollars? _____
2. Would you give any to charity? If yes, which ones? _____
3. Would you give money to anyone? Who? _____
4. What would you buy for yourself? _____
5. Would you save any of the money? Why? _____

B Write a paragraph about having a million dollars. Use the answers in Part A to help you.

If I had a million dollars, I'd ...

Dreams and Reality

Unit 8 Review

Language chart review

If clauses with could ... would	Infinitives to give a reason
If I could learn any language, I**'d learn** Japanese. **If he could change the way he looks**, he**'d be** taller.	I'm going to be a detective. I want to solve mysteries. I'm going to be a detective **to solve** mysteries. She wants to be a carpenter. She wants to make furniture. She wants to be a carpenter **to make** furniture.

A Look at the pictures. Then write sentences about the people's dreams with the words in the box.

☐ buy anything: video arcade – play games all day
☐ have any job in the world: be an astronaut – travel in outer space
☐ play any sport: soccer – score a lot of goals
☑ visit any city in the world: Paris – see the Eiffel Tower

1. *If she could visit any city in the world, she'd visit Paris. She wants to visit Paris to see the Eiffel Tower.*

2. _____

3. _____

4. _____

Language chart review

Unreal conditional with *if* clauses

What **would** you **do if** you **found** an expensive ring on the street?
If I **found** an expensive ring on the street, **I'd give** it to the police.
I'd give it to the police.

Indefinite pronouns

Questions	Negative statements	Affirmative statements
Have you done **anything** crazy?	I haven't done **anything** crazy.	I did **something** crazy.
Have you been **anywhere** fun?	I haven't been **anywhere** fun.	I went **somewhere** fun.
Did you meet **anyone** special?	I didn't meet **anyone** special.	I met **someone** very special.

B Complete the conversations.

1. **A** What <u>would you do</u> (you / do) if <u>you saw</u> (you / see) a snake?
   B <u>I'd scream</u> (I / scream)!

2. **A** If _____ (someone / ask) me to give him the answers to a test,
   _____ (I / say) no. What _____ (you / do)?
   B _____ (I / say) no, too. Do you think _____ (you / tell) the teacher?
   A No, _____ (I / not tell) the teacher. _____ (I / tell) the principal!

C Complete the book review with *anything, something, anyone, someone, anywhere,* or *somewhere*.

Have you read <u>anything</u> interesting this month? Well, I have _____ fun and fascinating for you. It's *How to Be Someone Special,* Melissa Costa's new book for teens. I haven't read _____ as interesting as this in a long time. I don't know _____ who doesn't like this book. The writer tells us we don't have to go _____ unusual or do _____ fascinating to be happy. We just have to use our imaginations! Go _____ quiet and read this book. Then give it to _____ special.

Take another look!

Circle T (true) or F (false).

1. In the sentence "If I found a lot of money, I'd keep it," 'd is the contraction for *would*.   T   F

2. Questions with "What would you do if . . . ?" are asking about things that can never happen.   T   F

Dreams and Reality 113

Unit 1 Game Memory game

A What were these people doing one hot afternoon last summer at one o'clock? Look at the picture for two minutes. Then close your book, and write six questions and answers about the picture on a separate piece of paper. Open your book and check your answers.

B Work with a classmate. Close your books and put away your papers. Take turns asking your questions. Who remembers the most?

You Were Angelina and Mark playing volleyball?
Classmate No, they weren't. They were playing basketball.
You You're correct.

Classmate What was Mrs. Harper doing?
You She was talking on her cell phone.
Classmate That's right.

Unit 2 — Game What will happen?

What will you do before you graduate from high school? Play the game with a classmate. Use things in your bag as game markers. Use a coin to find out how many spaces to move. Heads = 1, Tails = 2.

Rules:
- Take turns. Flip a coin and move your marker to the correct space. Your classmate asks a question with the cue in the space. You answer, using *will*.

   Classmate 1 *Will you travel to a different country before you graduate from high school?*
   Classmate 2 *Yes, I'll travel to Chile before I graduate from high school.*

▶ No mistakes? Stay on that space.
◀ Mistakes? Move back one space.
- On a "free space," ask your classmate any question.
- The person who gets to FINISH first, wins.

START → travel to a different country → get better grades → learn a new sport → win a prize at school → **FREE SPACE** → get a summer job → You'll fail a test. Go back 3 spaces. → perform on stage → see a famous person → move to another city → speak English well → You'll make a new friend. Move ahead 3 spaces. → Take another turn. → try a new food → study in another country → go to a rock concert → Move your marker to your classmate's space. → get a new pet → **FINISH**

Unit 3 Game — Invitations, permission, and requests

A Play the game with a classmate. Classmate 1 is *X*. Classmate 2 is *O*.

Classmate 1 Choose any space. Follow the instructions. Ask Classmate 2 a question.

Classmate 2 Answer the question. Say *yes* or *no*.

Classmate 1 Was the question correct? Mark the box in the space with an *X*. Did you make a mistake? Do not mark the box in the space.

Classmate 2 Take your turn. Choose a different space and ask Classmate 1 a question.

Continue playing until all spaces have been marked. The person with the most *X*s or *O*s is the winner.

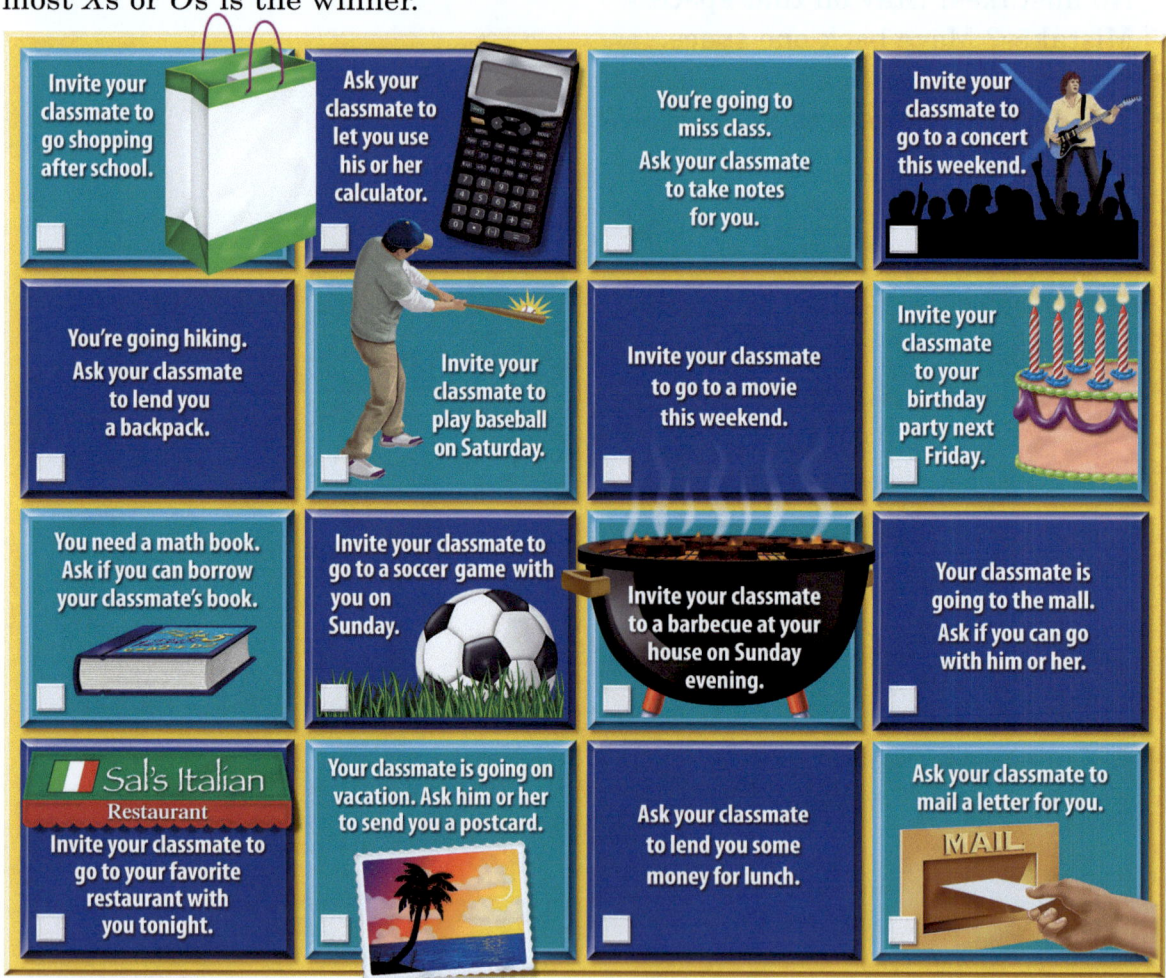

B Choose two spaces you did not ask questions about. Write questions and answers.

1. **Q:** _____
   A: _____
2. **Q:** _____
   A: _____

Unit 4 Game Guess the person

Read about these teens. Then play a guessing game with a classmate. Take turns.

Classmate 1 Choose a teen below. Pretend to be that person. Don't tell Classmate 2 who it is. Answer Classmate 2's questions.
Classmate 2 Classmate 1 is pretending to be a teen below. Try to guess who. Ask questions.

Classmate 2 Do you like chatting online?
Classmate 1 Yes, I do.
Classmate 2 Are you outgoing?
Classmate 1 Yes, I am.
Classmate 2 Is drawing pictures your hobby?
Classmate 1 Yes, it is.
Classmate 2 You're Kwan!

Jane: I enjoy writing e-mails to friends. Collecting comic books is my hobby. I like going to rock concerts. I'm outgoing.

Andre: I'm organized. I enjoy speaking French. I like drawing pictures. I'm creative. Chatting online is my favorite free-time activity.

Ana: Writing e-mail messages to my friends is my favorite free-time activity. I enjoy dancing. I'm hardworking. I like playing baseball.

Kwan: I like chatting online. Drawing pictures is my hobby. I enjoy listening to rock music. I'm outgoing.

Ryan: I enjoy talking on the phone with my friends. I'm creative. I enjoy writing stories about life in the future. I'm trustworthy. When I make a promise, I keep it. Playing soccer is my favorite free-time activity.

Elena: I enjoy speaking French. I like talking on the phone with friends. Dancing is my favorite free-time activity. I'm hardworking. I spend a lot of time on homework and chores.

Sophie: I enjoy listening to rap music. Collecting comic books is my hobby. I'm outgoing. Playing soccer is my favorite sports activity.

Gabriel: I enjoy playing baseball. I'm trustworthy. When I promise to do something, I do it. Listening to rap music is my favorite free-time activity. I'm organized.

Unit 5 Game Crossword puzzle

A Complete the story with the past participles of the verbs in the box. Then complete the puzzle.

☐ act ☐ do ☐ hang ☐ meet ☐ rent ☐ travel
☐ be ☐ go ☐ make ☐ read ☐ sing ☐ win

Hi, I'm Hank. I've **[7 down]** _____ really busy this year. Here are some of the things I've **[4 down]** _____ . I love reading science fiction. I've **[8 down]** _____ 40 science fiction books this year. I love movies, too. I've **[3 down]** _____ about 60 DVDs. I play soccer on my school's team, but we haven't **[2 across]** _____ any games this year. I've **[12 across]** _____ in three concerts with a singing group at school. I'm in the drama club, and I've **[11 across]** _____ in two plays. With all of these activities, I've **[9 down]** _____ a lot of people, and I've **[6 down]** _____ some great friends. I've also **[10 across]** _____ a lot this year. I've **[5 across]** _____ to three different countries, but I haven't **[1 down]** _____ out at the mall with my friends. We're all too busy for that!

B Work with a classmate. Make sentences about what you've done this year. Each person writes as many sentences as possible in two minutes using the past participles in Part A. Who wrote the most correct sentences?

Game Guessing game

A Play the game with a classmate. Take turns.

- Do not look at the chart below. For one minute, talk to a classmate about some fun or unusual things you've done. Use *I've*.
- Now look at the activities in the chart. Check (✓) the activities you have never done. Then check (✓) the activities you think your classmate has never done.
- Ask your classmate about the activities in the chart.
  Use *Have you ever . . . ?* For example: *Have you ever eaten chocolate ants?*
- Circle each of your classmate's answers that you guessed right.

	You	Your classmate
eat chocolate ants	☐	☐
go snorkeling	☐	☐
see an elephant	☐	☐
try Indian food	☐	☐
go to a fireworks show	☐	☐
climb a mountain	☐	☐
read a book in English	☐	☐
sing on a stage	☐	☐
play a musical instrument	☐	☐
have a pen pal in another country	☐	☐
travel to another city	☐	☐
explore a rain forest	☐	☐
ride a horse	☐	☐

Number of activities I circled: _____
Number of activities my classmate circled: _____

B Walk around the classroom. Find classmates who have done the activities in the chart below. Write their names and ask when they last did these activities.

Hi, Sergio. Have you ever chatted online?

Yes, I have.

When did you last chat online?

Two weeks ago.

	Name	When
chat online	Sergio	two weeks ago
speak English at home		
cook a meal		
go to a rock concert		
get 100 percent on a test		

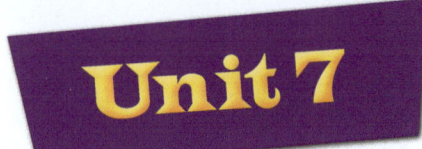

Unit 7 Game Mark the space

A Play the game with a classmate. Classmate 1 is *X*. Classmate 2 is *O*.

Classmate 1 Choose any space. Make statements using the words as cues.

My cousin's cat is the cutest cat I've ever seen.

▶ Is the statement correct? Mark the box in the space with an *X*.

◀ Not correct? Do not mark the box in the space.

Classmate 2 Take your turn.

Continue playing until all spaces have been marked. The person with the most *X*s or *O*s is the winner.

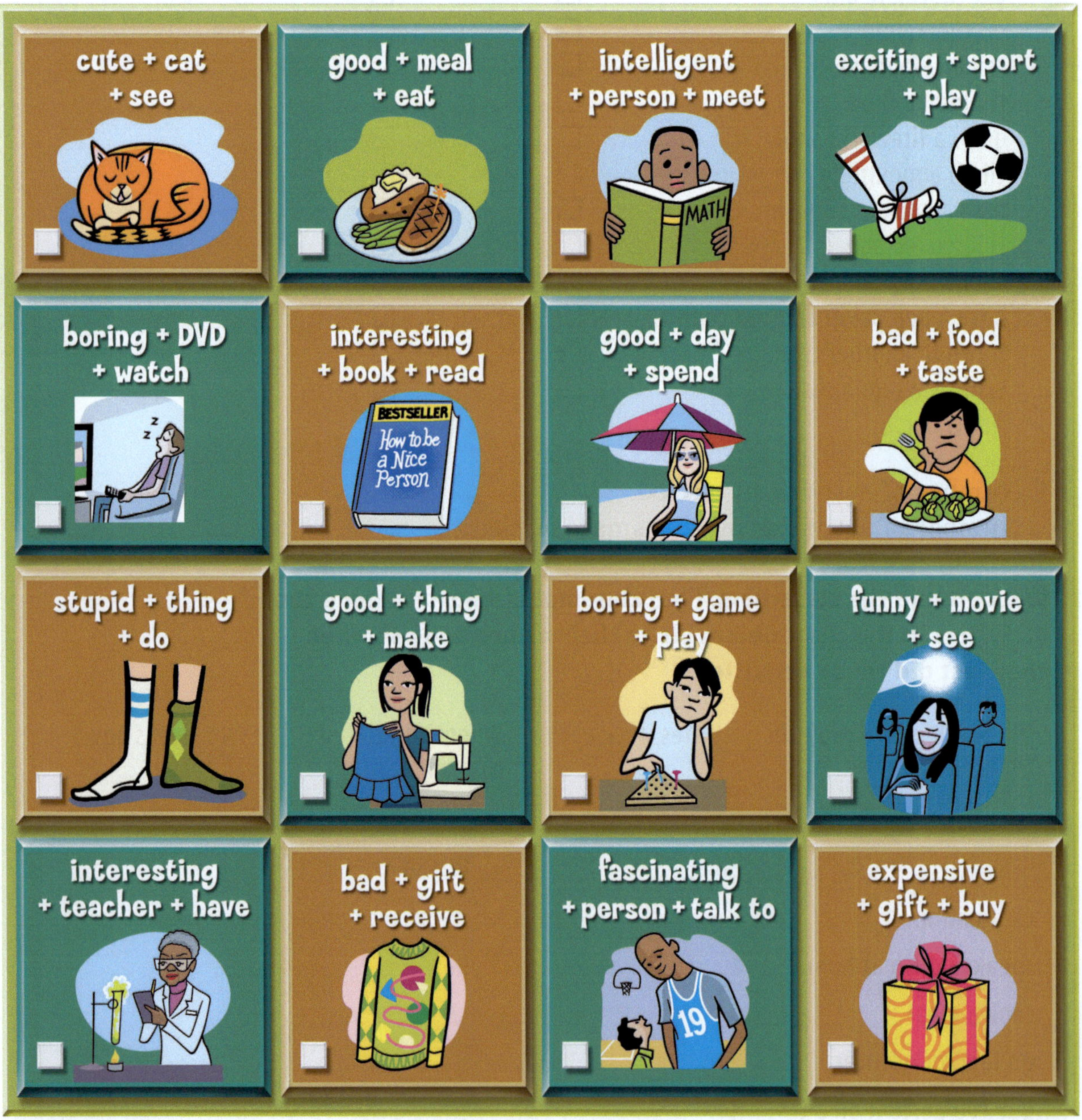

cute + cat + see
good + meal + eat
intelligent + person + meet
MATH
exciting + sport + play
boring + DVD + watch
interesting + book + read
BESTSELLER
How to be a Nice Person
good + day + spend
bad + food + taste
stupid + thing + do
good + thing + make
boring + game + play
funny + movie + see
interesting + teacher + have
bad + gift + receive
fascinating + person + talk to
19
expensive + gift + buy

Unit 8 Game: What would you do if . . . ?

Play the game with a classmate. Use things in your bag as game markers. Use a coin to find out how many spaces to move. Heads = 1, Tails = 2.

Rules:
- Take turns. Flip a coin and move your marker to the correct space. Follow the directions or ask a question with *What would you do if . . . ?* and the cue in the space. Your classmate answers the question.
  Classmate 1 *What would you do if you found an expensive ring on the street?*
  Classmate 2 *I'd take it to my parents.*
  ▶ Classmate 1, no mistakes? Stay in that space.
  ◀ Classmate 1, mistakes? Move back one space.
- The person who gets to FINISH first, wins.

START → You find an expensive ring on the street. → You see someone littering. → Move ahead one space. → You see someone steal a CD from a store. → Lose a turn. → You forget your homework at home. → You get extra money back in a store. → Take another turn. → You need to pay at a restaurant, but you have no money. → Someone you don't like invites you to his or her birthday party. → You forget a friend's birthday. → You win a bicycle in a contest. → Move back two spaces. → Your best friend tells you a secret. → You get a guitar as a gift, but you don't play. → Move back two spaces. → You get lost in the woods. → Your cell phone rings in a movie theater. → **FINISH**

Get Connected Vocabulary Practice

Unit 1

Complete the advertisement with the words in the box.

☐ best-loved (adj.)   ☑ gymnast (n.)   ☐ scrapbook (n.)   ☐ train (v.)

Be a Champion!

Would you like to be a top ___gymnast___? Would you like to _____ with the sport's top coaches? Become a winner at Champion's Gymnastics Center! We have classes for children of all ages and levels. You can see pictures of all of our gymnastics stars in our online _____. Find out why gymnastics is one of America's _____ sports. The center is open Monday to Saturday from 9:00 a.m. to 5:00 p.m.

Unit 2

Complete the sentences with the words in the box.

☐ certain (adj.)   ☐ cure (v.)   ☑ flying (adj.)   ☐ gas (n.)   ☐ headlines (n.)   ☐ medicines (n.)

1. I had a crazy dream about a ___flying___ bicycle. I was riding it in the air!
2. I don't always have time to read all of the newspaper, but I try to look at the _____.
3. My grandmother is 100 years old and takes many different _____.
4. You should try some chicken soup when you have a cold. It can help _____ it.
5. He might go to the party, but he's not _____.
6. I don't have enough _____ in my car, so let's take your car.

Unit 3

Match the words to the correct meanings.

1. texting (n.) _f_
2. convenient (adj.) ____
3. e-vite (n.) ____
4. fuzzy (adj.) ____
5. firm (adj.) ____
6. social networking Web site (n.) ____

a. not sure
b. an online "meeting" place
c. very sure
d. an online invitation
e. easy or useful
f. sending messages from a cell phone

Unit 4

Complete the sentences with the words in the box.

☐ birth order (n.)   ☐ firstborn (adj.)   ☐ middle (adj.)   ☐ researchers (n.)
☐ boss (n.)   ☑ leaders (n.)   ☐ peace (n.)

1. The city's _leaders_ are hard-working, organized people.
2. _____ have discovered cures for many sicknesses.
3. John is the oldest child in his family. He's the _____ child.
4. My father owns a successful business. He's the _____ .
5. Julie is the _____ child. She's younger than Mary and older than Dave.
6. World _____ should be important to everyone.
7. Knowing a friend's _____ can help you understand his or her personality.

Unit 5

Complete the sentences with the words in the box.

☐ audition (n.) ☐ comedian (n.) ☑ reality show (n.) ☐ viewers (n.)
☐ career (n.) ☐ go ahead (v.) ☐ recording contract (n.)

1. That dancing __reality show__ isn't very interesting, so I don't watch it.
2. I saw that _____ on TV last night and he was very funny.
3. Being a doctor is a great _____ because you help people.
4. _____ and try that math problem. It's really easy!
5. His _____ was really bad so they didn't ask him to be on the show.
6. That show is really popular. It has more _____ than any other TV show this year.
7. Chris Daughtry didn't win a _____ on *American Idol*, but he's still very successful.

Unit 6

Circle the correct words to complete the sentences.

1. My sister made this (stunt / (bowl)) in her art class.
2. We didn't know Jim could play the piano so well.
   We were (disappointed / amazed).
3. The cat climbed up the (pole / bowl) and couldn't get down.
4. He likes to do amazing (audiences / stunts). Last month, he stayed in a very small room with no sleep for four days.
5. The artist made a sculpture from a (block / pole) of ice.

124 **Get Connected Vocabulary Practice**

Unit 7

Complete the sentences with the words in the box.

> ☐ community work (n.) ☐ memorable (adj.) ☐ wilderness skills (n.)
> ☑ farmers (n.) ☐ pandas (n.)

1. When there is no rain, ____farmers____ can't grow vegetables.
2. The teens in our school do a lot of _____ .
3. _____ are important if you like to hike and camp for a week in forests.
4. All my family is here. This is the most _____ birthday party I've ever had.
5. There aren't as many _____ in China as there were 10 years ago.

Unit 8

Complete the advertisement with the words in the box.

> ☐ ambassador (n.) ☐ cancer (n.) ☐ education (n.) ☑ role (n.)
> ☐ billion (adj.) ☐ celebrities (n.) ☐ foundation's (n.)

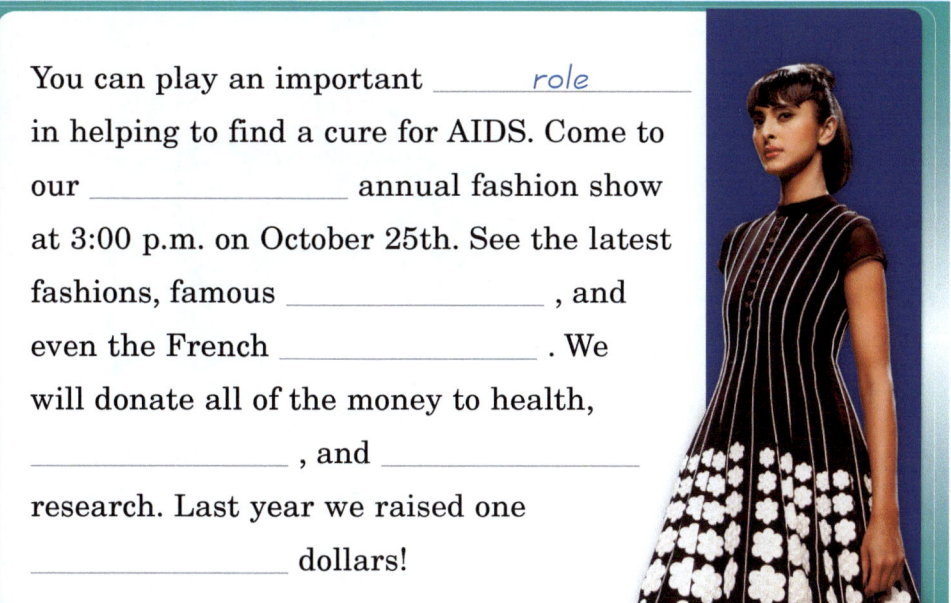

You can play an important ____role____ in helping to find a cure for AIDS. Come to our _____ annual fashion show at 3:00 p.m. on October 25th. See the latest fashions, famous _____ , and even the French _____ . We will donate all of the money to health, _____ , and _____ research. Last year we raised one _____ dollars!

Unit 1

Theme Project: Make a group booklet about people who make a difference.
Theme: Citizenship; environmentalism
Goal: To learn more about people who help other people, animals, or the earth

At Home

Read about a young man who has helped wildlife and nature.

> Jeff Howard is in the 11th grade in Ontario, Canada. He's an environmentalist. He loves wildlife and nature. When he was growing up, while other kids were playing computer games, texting, or talking to friends, Jeff helped to preserve nature and wildlife. He cleaned streams, counted birds, and rescued wild animals. He received awards for his work. Jeff really loves water birds. Once when he was out on a lake, Jeff saw a man being unkind to an injured swan. Jeff took a picture and reported the man to the police. His mom says, "We need youth to be interested and involved in nature."

Think of a person who has helped other people, animals, or the earth. Complete the chart. Use your dictionary and the Internet, if necessary.

Name: _____
Special activity: _____
Age when this person
started the special activity: _____
Other information: _____

Draw a picture or bring a photo of the person to class.

In Class

1. Make a page of your person. Use the sample booklet page as a model.

2. Tell your group about your person.

   > This is Marcelo Duarte. When he was eight, he started collecting books and . . .

3. Make a group booklet. Make a cover for your booklet. Then staple together all of your pages and the cover to make your booklet.

4. Pass around the booklets. Which person made the greatest difference?

Name: Marcelo Duarte
Special activity: Collecting books and giving them to poor children
Age when he started: 8
Other: He was on a famous TV show.

Sample booklet page

Theme Project: Make a bookmark about your future.
Theme: Ethics and citizenship; diversity
Goal: To think about and share information about the future

At Home

Read about Griffin's ideas about his future.

Griffin Stevens is 13 years old and goes to Saint Ann's School in Brooklyn, New York. This is what he thinks about his future:
- I'll do well in my classes.
- I'm going to work hard on my soccer and basketball skills.
- I'll probably join the high school soccer team.
- I probably won't become a professional athlete.
- I might go to a very good college.

What do you think you will or won't do in your future? Write three of your ideas. Use your dictionary, if necessary.

1. _____
2. _____
3. _____

Draw a picture or bring a photo of yourself to class.

In Class

1. **Make a bookmark. Do not put your picture or photo on it. Use the sample bookmark as a model.**

2. **Put all the bookmarks and the pictures or photos in the center of your group. Choose a bookmark that isn't yours and read the information to your group. The other group members guess the person. Finally, put the correct pictures or photos on the bookmarks.**

> This person won't become an architect. This person might try out for . . .

> Is it Oren?

3. **Display the bookmarks in your classroom. Walk around and look at all of them. How many ideas were the same as yours?**

I won't become an architect.
I might try out for a sports team.
I probably won't quit my part-time job.

Sample bookmark

Unit 2 Theme Project 127

Unit 3

Theme Project: Make fact cards about an environmental issue.
Theme: The environment and its preservation
Goal: To share information about ways to help the environment

At Home

Read about ways to save the environment.

> People are chopping down too many trees. If we don't stop cutting down trees, many animals will die because they won't have a place to live. There are many ways that you can help save trees.
> - Recycle your paper.
> - Use recycled paper products.
> - Send e-greetings. Don't send paper cards.
> - Take your own bags to stores when you go shopping.
> - Don't use paper plates or cups.

Think of an environmental problem and how to solve it. Complete the chart.
Use your dictionary or the Internet, if necessary.

Describe the problem: _____
Result of the problem: _____
Solution to the problem: _____

Draw a picture or bring a photo that shows the problem to class.

In Class

1. Make a card about your environmental problem. Use the sample card as a model.

2. Tell your group about your problem.

   > My problem is our air is dirty. If we don't clean the air, more people and animals will get sick, and . . .

3. Choose a group leader. Present your cards to another group.

4. Display the fact cards in your classroom. Walk around and look at all of them. What problem did most people choose?

Our air is dirty.
If we don't clean the air, more people and animals will get sick, and more plants will die.
- Walk or bicycle to places. Don't go by bus or car.
- Use machines that don't use gas – like a lawnmower you push.
- Use fans, not air conditioners.

Sample fact card

Unit 4

Theme Project: Make a group personality profile booklet.
Theme: Citizenship; cultural diversity
Goal: To create stronger relationships within your classroom community

At Home

Read the personality profiles of two teens.

> I'm Diego. I'm outgoing and very hardworking. I like making new friends. I love spending time outdoors – hiking, kayaking, and playing soccer. I enjoy playing computer games and chatting online, too. I don't like cleaning my room.

> My name is Carla. I'm kind, thoughtful, and trustworthy, and I'm a little shy. I don't like playing sports very much. I have a Web site, and I write a blog. I like taking pictures with my digital camera and editing them online.

Write a personality profile. Complete the chart. Use your dictionary, if necessary.

My name: _____
My personality: _____
Things I like doing: _____
Things I don't like doing: _____

Draw a picture or bring a photo of yourself to class.

In Class

1. Make a profile page. Use the sample booklet page as a model.
2. Present your profile to your group.

   > I'm creative and independent. I like . . .

3. Make a group booklet. Make a cover for your booklet. Then staple together all of your pages and the cover to make your booklet.
4. Choose a group leader. The group leader reads the personality profiles, and the other group members guess the student.
5. Pass around the booklets. Which two classmates have the most in common?

I'm creative and independent. I like hanging out with my friends. I don't like doing chores.

Sample booklet page

Unit 5

Theme Project: Make a cross-cultural experiences poster.
Theme: Multiculturalism
Goal: To create stronger relationships in your classroom community

At Home

Read about cross-cultural experiences.

It's important to know about other cultures and other people, and you don't need to travel to another country to do this. Have you ever talked to someone who doesn't speak your language? Have you ever eaten food from another country? Have you ever seen a foreign movie on TV? Maybe you've read books about people in other countries or have chatted with people from other countries online. If you've done any of these things, you have learned something about another culture and had a cross-cultural experience.

Think of cross-cultural experiences you have had. Complete the sentences. Use the ideas in the box or your own ideas. Use your dictionary, if necessary.

1. I have _____.
2. I have _____.
3. I have _____.
4. I have _____.

books	movies
food	online
friend	travel
in school	TV

Draw a picture or bring a photo of one or more of the experiences to class.

In Class

- Look at all the experiences. Choose one experience for each group member.
- Make a poster. Use the sample poster as a model.
- Choose a group leader. Present your poster to another group.

> Megumi has visited Colombia. Bruno has . . .

- Display the posters in your classroom. Walk around and look at all of them. Which group has had the most interesting cross-cultural experiences?

① Megumi has visited Colombia.
② Bruno has made international friends online.
③ Carlo's family has had a homestay student at their house.
④ Eduardo has studied three languages.

Sample poster

Unit 6

Theme Project: Make a booklet about amazing people.
Theme: Multiculturalism; citizenship
Goal: To learn more about a person who has done amazing things

At Home

Read about an amazing nine-year-old boy.

> Jordan Hawk is nine years old and plays the piano very well. He also writes songs. He has already composed 20 piano pieces and has recorded a DVD. He has also given many live concerts.
>
> Jordan started playing the piano when he was three, and he started composing his own pieces when he was five. He has been on several TV shows. He speaks two languages – English and Russian. He hasn't learned Spanish yet, but he wants to.

Think of an amazing person. It can be someone you know. Complete the chart. Use your dictionary or the Internet, if necessary.

Name	What has he or she already done?	What has he or she not done yet?

Draw a picture or bring a photo of the person to class.

In Class

1. **Make a page of your person. Use the sample booklet page as a model.**
2. **Tell your group about your person.**

   > My brother, Jim, is amazing. He has . . .

3. **Make a group booklet. Make a cover for your booklet. Then staple together all of your pages and the cover to make your booklet.**
4. **Display the booklets in your classroom. Walk around and look at all of them. Vote on the most amazing person.**

> My brother, Jim, is amazing. He has already learned three languages. He has played on the school soccer team for five years, and has scored a lot of goals. He hasn't finished high school yet. He hasn't traveled to another country yet, but he wants to.

Sample booklet page

Theme Project: Make a poster about group preferences.
Theme: Cultural diversity
Goal: To share ideas about preferences

At Home

Read about parents' preferences about schools.

> Some parents in the U.S. don't want to send their children to a regular school. They think that homeschooling is better than studying in a regular school. There are about 2 million children in the U.S. who are homeschooled. Parents think that the best thing about homeschooling is that it creates a closer relationship with their children.

Choose one of these topics: sports, music, pets, or TV shows. Complete the chart. Then write sentences about your preferences. Use your dictionary, if necessary.

Like a lot	Like	Like a little	Don't like	Don't like at all

I like _____ a lot. _____

_____

Draw pictures or bring photos of your topic to class.

In Class

- Present your preferences to your group.

  > I like soccer. I think it's the most interesting sport to play. I don't like . . .

- Make a poster for the topics in your group. Use the sample poster as a model.
- Choose a group leader. Present your poster to another group.

  > Luis and Selma don't like tennis at all. They think . . .

- Display the posters in your classroom. Walk around and look at all of them. Who had the same ideas as you?

Sample poster

Unit 8

Theme Project: Make a group booklet showing how you could help others with $5,000.

Theme: Citizenship; consumerism

Goal: To learn about the needs of different people and charities

At Home

Read about a show to help people.

> Oprah Winfrey is a famous TV star. In 2008 she had a special show, a reality show, called *Oprah's Big Give*. The goal of the show was to help people, and the person who helped the most was the winner. In each show, contestants went to a different U.S. city. They received money and a task they had to do. Sometimes they did the task alone, and sometimes they did it in pairs or groups. Sometimes they were told who to help, and other times they had to find people in need. At the end of each show, judges decided who spent the money in the most helpful way. At the end of the TV series, the winner got $1 million ($500,000 for themselves, and $500,000 to give away).

What would you do to help people? Write four sentences beginning with *If I had $5,000, I'd . . .* . Use your dictionary, if necessary.

1. _____
2. _____
3. _____
4. _____

Draw pictures or bring photos of your ideas to class.

In Class

- Tell your group about your ideas.

    > If I had $5,000, I'd buy food for people . . .

- Choose one idea from each group member.
- Make a page of your idea. Use the sample booklet page as a model.
- Make a group booklet. Make a cover for your booklet. Then staple together all of your pages and the cover to make your booklet.
- Pass around the booklets. Vote on the booklet with the most helpful ideas.

Meg:
If I had $5,000, I'd buy food for people who live on the street, and I'd give it to them.

Sample booklet page

Verb List

Verbs are listed with the page number on which they first appear.

Regular Verbs

Present	Past	Participle	Page
act	acted	acted	4
agree	agreed	agreed	98
amaze	amazed	amazed	30
answer	answered	answered	12
appear	appeared	appeared	61
arrive	arrived	arrived	39
ask	asked	asked	14
audition	auditioned	auditioned	68
backpack	backpacked	backpacked	24
behave	behaved	behaved	80
believe	believed	believed	38
borrow	borrowed	borrowed	32
call	called	called	40
camp	camped	camped	2
celebrate	celebrated	celebrated	66
change	changed	changed	68
chat	chatted	chatted	44
cheat	cheated	cheated	102
clean	cleaned	cleaned	16
climb	climbed	climbed	63
close	closed	closed	33
collect	collected	collected	50
compete	competed	competed	61
connect	connected	connected	16
cook	cooked	cooked	16
copy	copied	copied	102
crawl	crawled	crawled	14
create	created	created	106
cure	cured	cured	26
dance	danced	danced	42
decide	decided	decided	23
depend	depended	depended	36
describe	described	described	82
design	designed	designed	4
disappear	disappeared	disappeared	82
discover	discovered	discovered	54
donate	donated	donated	110
download	downloaded	downloaded	44
drop	dropped	dropped	98
dye	dyed	dyed	72
eavesdrop	eavesdropped	eavesdropped	102
edit	edited	edited	22
e-mail	e-mailed	e-mailed	2
enjoy	enjoyed	enjoyed	12
enter	entered	entered	102
entertain	entertained	entertained	17
erase	erased	erased	89
exercise	exercised	exercised	10
expect	expected	expected	30
experience	experienced	experienced	96

Present	Past	Participle	Page
explain	explained	explained	14
explore	explored	explored	30
film	filmed	filmed	2
finish	finished	finished	18
fix	fixed	fixed	29
gossip	gossiped	gossiped	102
graduate	graduated	graduated	18
guess	guessed	guessed	73
happen	happened	happened	3
hate	hated	hated	43
head	headed	headed	30
help	helped	helped	8
hike	hiked	hiked	2
homeschool	homeschooled	homeschooled	78
hope	hoped	hoped	36
invite	invited	invited	42
jaywalk	jaywalked	jaywalked	102
join	joined	joined	4
jump	jumped	jumped	73
laugh	laughed	laughed	68
learn	learned	learned	4
lie	lied	lied	102
like	liked	liked	2
listen	listened	listened	12
litter	littered	littered	102
live	lived	lived	17
look	looked	looked	10
love	loved	loved	4
marry	married	married	81
matter	mattered	mattered	103
move	moved	moved	8
need	needed	needed	21
open	opened	opened	16
order	ordered	ordered	34
pack	packed	packed	38
pass	passed	passed	18
perform	performed	performed	8
pick	picked	picked	103
play	played	played	3
practice	practiced	practiced	6
push	pushed	pushed	8
rain	rained	rained	14
receive	received	received	62
record	recorded	recorded	60
relax	relaxed	relaxed	12
remember	remembered	remembered	46
rent	rented	rented	37
replace	replaced	replaced	16
report	reported	reported	106
rescue	rescued	rescued	30
return	returned	returned	30
review	reviewed	reviewed	80
save	saved	saved	30
scream	screamed	screamed	113
seem	seemed	seemed	12
share	shared	shared	18
shop	shopped	shopped	16
sign	signed	signed	23
skateboard	skateboarded	skateboarded	34
snorkel	snorkeled	snorkeled	38

Present	Past	Participle	Page
solve	solved	solved	106
sound	sounded	sounded	6
star	starred	starred	81
start	started	started	5
stay	stayed	stayed	2
stop	stopped	stopped	7
study	studied	studied	3
support	supported	supported	60
suppose	supposed	supposed	31
surprise	surprised	surprised	30
survive	survived	survived	110
talk	talked	talked	42
test	tested	tested	30
text	texted	texted	40
train	trained	trained	12
travel	traveled	traveled	2
trespass	trespassed	trespassed	102
try	tried	tried	7
turn	turned	turned	79
type	typed	typed	21
use	used	used	10
vacation	vacationed	vacationed	79
visit	visited	visited	2
wait	waited	waited	6
walk	walked	walked	14
want	wanted	wanted	3
watch	watched	watched	3
welcome	welcomed	welcomed	92
work	worked	worked	3
worry	worried	worried	30

Irregular Verbs

Present	Past	Participle	Page
babysit	babysat	babysat	31
be	was	been	2
become	became	become	2
break	broke	broken	3
bring	brought	brought	22
buy	bought	bought	17
come	came	come	15
cut	cut	cut	34
do	did	done	3
draw	drew	drawn	93
drink	drank	drunk	28
drive	drove	driven	7
eat	ate	eaten	3
fall	fell	fallen	9
feed	fed	fed	21
fly	flew	flown	37
forget	forgot	forgotten	31
get	got	gotten	2
give	gave	given	8
go	went	gone	2
hang	hung	hung	2
have	had	had	2
hear	heard	heard	14
hit	hit	hit	3

Present	Past	Participle	Page
hurt	hurt	hurt	83
keep	kept	kept	46
know	knew	known	10
leave	left	left	30
let	let	let	33
lose	lost	lost	2
make	made	made	2
pay	paid	paid	25
put	put	put	3
read	read	read	14
ride	rode	ridden	6
ring	rang	rung	15
run	ran	run	34
say	said	said	12
see	saw	seen	2
sell	sold	sold	61
send	sent	sent	40
set	set	set	78
show	showed	shown	66
sing	sang	sung	60
sit	sat	sat	22
sleep	slept	slept	7
speak	spoke	spoken	17
spend	spent	spent	2
stand	stood	stood	14
swim	swam	swum	34
take	took	taken	2
teach	taught	taught	50
tell	told	told	14
think	thought	thought	6
throw	threw	thrown	103
understand	understood	understood	41
wake	woke	woken	7
wear	wore	worn	10
win	won	won	8
write	wrote	written	12

Word List

This list includes the key words and phrases in *Connect, Second Edition* Student's Book 4. The numbers next to each word are the page numbers on which the words first appear.

Key Vocabulary

Aa
abroad (18) _____
absolutely not (33) _____
act (4) _____
afraid (47) _____
Africa (71) _____
album (62) _____
alike (47) _____
all over (2) _____
all right (32) _____
amaze (30) _____
amazed (82) _____
ambassador (110) _____
angry (46) _____
Antarctica (108) _____
anyone (14) _____
anyplace (101) _____
appear (61) _____
appearance (53) _____
article (22) _____
as (much) as (92) _____
astronaut (57) _____
at all (29) _____
audience (60) _____
audition (68) _____
autograph (60) _____
award (9) _____

Bb
backpack [verb] (24) _____
backstage (64) _____
bad dream (16) _____
badminton (22) _____
bad-tempered (42) _____
ballroom dancing class (22) _____
basketball team (9) _____
battery (21) _____
behave (80) _____
behavior (102) _____
below (17) _____
best-loved (12) _____
better than (50) _____
billion (110) _____
birth order (54) _____
block (102) _____
board game (45) _____
book report (38) _____
borrow (32) _____

boss (54) _____
bowl (82) _____
boyfriend (52) _____
brand-new (30) _____
broken (32) _____
butterfly (51) _____

Cc
campground (2) _____
campsite (7) _____
cancer (110) _____
can't stand [hate] (86) _____
career (68) _____
carelessly (102) _____
carpenter (106) _____
cartoon (11) _____
cartoon artist (51) _____
cave tour (30) _____
celebrity (110) _____
cellist (60) _____
cello (60) _____
center (66) _____
certain (26) _____
champion [adjective] (8) _____
champion [noun] (8) _____
charity (60) _____
cheat (102) _____
choice (94) _____
circus school (50) _____
close (33) _____
collect (11) _____
collection (5) _____
college (18) _____
college degree (79) _____
color TV (67) _____
come back (30) _____
comedian (68) _____
commercials (15) _____
community work (96) _____
company (67) _____
compass (2) _____
compete (61) _____
competition (8) _____
computer course (5) _____
computer file (89) _____
computer game (4) _____
computer programmer (106) _____
computer programming (24) _____

computer science (81) _____
connect (16) _____
contact lenses (10) _____
continent (16) _____
convenient (26) _____
conversation (102) _____
cooking (93) _____
cooking class (22) _____
copy (62) _____
country tour (39) _____
couple [a couple of] (24) _____
crab (109) _____
crawl (14) _____
creative (46) _____
credit card (17) _____
crocodile meat (88) _____
cure (26) _____
cut (34) _____

Dd
decide on (79) _____
definitely (25) _____
depend on [it depends on] (36) _____
design [noun] (3) _____
design [verb] (3) _____
detective (106) _____
digital camera (32) _____
discovery (106) _____
disgusting (88) _____
do the dishes (86) _____
download (44) _____
dream [noun] (18) _____
driver's license (18) _____
during (88) _____
DVD player (33) _____
dye [verb] (72) _____

Ee
easygoing (33) _____
eavesdrop (102) _____
ecological tour (77) _____
Ecuador (3) _____
edit (22) _____
education (110) _____
e-mail [verb] (2) _____
entertain (17) _____
entertainer (60) _____
erase (89) _____

138   Word List

Europe (24) _____
evening [adjective] (32) _____
event (101) _____
ever (64) _____
e-vite (40) _____
exchange program (75) _____
expect (30) _____
explain (14) _____
explore (30) _____
extra (6) _____

Ff
fall off (9) _____
fan club (5) _____
fan letter (64) _____
far away (18) _____
farmer (96) _____
fashion magazine (61) _____
fighter plane (101) _____
film [verb] (2) _____
fingerprints (21) _____
firm (40) _____
first-born (54) _____
fix (29) _____
flying (26) _____
for (66) _____
foreign (51) _____
for fun (48) _____
forgetful (46) _____
foundation (110) _____
frustrating (89) _____
furniture (106) _____
fuzzy (40) _____

Gg
garbage (102) _____
gas (26) _____
get back (38) _____
get home (39) _____
get married (18) _____
get together (38) _____
girlfriend (64) _____
glasses (10) _____
go ahead (68) _____
go-cart (30) _____
gold medal (8) _____
gossip (102) _____
graduate (18) _____
graduation (20) _____
grand opening (30) _____
ground (30) _____
gymnast (12) _____
gymnastics (5) _____

Hh
haircut (39) _____
happen (3) _____
hardworking (46) _____
head for (30) _____
headlines (26) _____
high school (18) _____

highway (7) _____
hit [adjective] (60) _____
hobbies (5) _____
hometown (2) _____
honest (46) _____
How long . . . (66) _____
human (16) _____
husband (18) _____

Ii
ice hotel (50) _____
if (16) _____
imagination (47) _____
in danger (30) _____
independent (46) _____
information (44) _____
in order (46) _____
in secret (102) _____
instant message (3) _____
intelligent (62) _____
international hotel (24) _____
interview (60) _____
invitation (35) _____
invite (42) _____
invited [get invited] (64) _____

Jj
jaywalk (102) _____
job [get a job] (18) _____
journalist (106) _____
judo (22) _____

Kk
karaoke (72) _____
karate class (58) _____
kind (93) _____

Ll
lazy (10) _____
leader (54) _____
lead singer (74) _____
lend (32) _____
let (33) _____
lie (102) _____
life event (8) _____
lightning (14) _____
lion tamer (50) _____
litter (102) _____
live [adjective] (60) _____
living space (18) _____
lots of (59) _____
luckily (2) _____

Mm
marathon (74) _____
marching band (22) _____
married (18) _____
marry (101) _____
martial arts classes (22) _____
match [sports] (8) _____
math whiz (78) _____

matter (103) _____
maybe (33) _____
mean [verb] (103) _____
medicine (19) _____
medicines (26) _____
memorable (96) _____
memory (71) _____
middle (54) _____
might (23) _____
might not (23) _____
million (60) _____
miniskirt (100) _____
moment (88) _____
Mongolia (104) _____
motorcycle (72) _____
mountain climbing (63) _____
movie crew (2) _____
movie industry (66) _____
musical instrument (9) _____
music lesson (4) _____
music show (11) _____

Nn
nightmare (16) _____
number (78) _____

Oo
of course (32) _____
office (23) _____
Olympic champion (51) _____
Olympic Games (61) _____
one-man band (50) _____
on stage (88) _____
on (your) own (107) _____
orchestra (8) _____
organized (46) _____
outdoor (36) _____
outer space (106) _____
outgoing (46) _____

Pp
pack (38) _____
paint (48) _____
panda (96) _____
paper (17) _____
parasailing (88) _____
pass (18) _____
peace (54) _____
permission (35) _____
personality (46) _____
personality type (46) _____
photographer (4) _____
photography club (4) _____
piano (6) _____
pick up (103) _____
poet (94) _____
poetry competition (108) _____
pole (82) _____
police (102) _____
pop culture (66) _____
possible (18) _____

prediction (16) _____
prince (101) _____
principal (113) _____
private (102) _____
probably (18) _____
professional [adjective] (8) _____
professor (16) _____
program [noun] (106) _____
promise [noun] (102) _____
put (3) _____
put up (7) _____

Rr
racing track (30) _____
racket club (22) _____
radio contest (64) _____
reading test (80) _____
reality show (68) _____
receive (65) _____
recently (51) _____
record [verb] (60) _____
recording contract (68) _____
recreation leader (22) _____
reflection (7) _____
relative (75) _____
replace (17) _____
report on (106) _____
reporter (22) _____
request (35) _____
researchers (54) _____
rescue (30) _____
return (30) _____
review (80) _____
rich (18) _____
right after (24) _____
risk (72) _____
road (14) _____
rock band (71) _____
rock-climbing [adjective] (73) _____
rock climbing [noun] (71) _____
rock concert (64) _____
rock star (20) _____
role (110) _____
royal family (101) _____
rumba (22) _____

Ss
samba (22) _____
save (30) _____
school newspaper (4) _____
school office (56) _____
school parade (22) _____
school play (4) _____
schoolwork (44) _____
science-fiction movie (86) _____
scrapbook (12) _____
scuba diving (75) _____

serious (93) _____
selection (90) _____
sharp [10:00 sharp] (32) _____
show [verb] (66) _____
sick (21) _____
sickness (21) _____
simple (78) _____
since (66) _____
singing competition (18) _____
site (3) _____
situation (101) _____
size (17) _____
skate park (58) _____
ski pants (39) _____
ski vacation (39) _____
skydiving (72) _____
sleeping machine (16) _____
sleep over [verb] (32) _____
snail (65) _____
snorkel (38) _____
snorkel gear (38) _____
snowboarding (93) _____
social networking Web site (40) _____
so far (58) _____
solve (106) _____
someday (4) _____
somewhere (42) _____
space (57) _____
sports scores (44) _____
spotlight (80) _____
star (66) _____
stay (2) _____
stay out (32) _____
stop by (38) _____
strict (33) _____
stuntman (82) _____
stunts (82) _____
successful (81) _____
summer school (3) _____
superhighway (16) _____
support (60) _____
surfing lessons (38) _____
Sweden (50) _____
sweet dream (16) _____

Tt
take off (30) _____
take risks (53) _____
talents (18) _____
talkative (92) _____
Teen Center (22) _____
tennis lesson (3) _____
tennis match (58) _____
tennis tournament (71) _____
test [verb] (30) _____
texting (40) _____
Thai food (76) _____
theater group (95) _____

though (58) _____
thoughtful (46) _____
thriller (87) _____
thunder (14) _____
tourist attraction (66) _____
track (30) _____
train [verb] (12) _____
trapeze (30) _____
trash (42) _____
trash can (103) _____
travel book (39) _____
trespass (102) _____
trustworthy (46) _____
twin (92) _____
twin brother (3) _____
try out (30) _____

Uu
understand (50) _____
unforgettable (88) _____
university (78) _____
used to (10) _____

Vv
vacation [verb] (79) _____
vacation plans (38) _____
veterinarian (106) _____
vice-president (57) _____
video camera (22) _____
viewers (68) _____
violin (11) _____
virtual reality ride (30) _____

Ww
weekend (30) _____
wet (14) _____
while (38) _____
wife (18) _____
wild [noun] (104) _____
wilderness skills (96) _____
will (16) _____
without (71) _____
won't (16) _____
World Cup (8) _____
worm (73) _____
worry (30) _____
worse (86) _____
worst [the worst] (86) _____
writer (18) _____

Yy
young (8) _____
yo-yo (78) _____

Acknowledgments

Connect, Second Edition has benefited from extensive development research. The authors and publishers would like to extend their particular thanks to all the CUP editorial, production, and marketing staff, as well as the following reviewers and consultants for their valuable insights and suggestions:

Focus Groups

São Paulo Suzi T. Almeida, Colégio Rio Branco; **Andreia C. Alves**, Colégio Guilherme de Almeida; **Patricia Del Valle**, Colégio I. L. Peretz; **Elaine Elia**, Centro de Educação Caminho Aberto; **Rosemilda L. Falletti**, Colégio Pio XII; **Amy Foot Gomes**, Instituto D. Placidina; **Lilian I. Leventhal**, Colégio I. L. Peretz; **Adriana Pellegrino**, Colégio Santo Agostinho; **Maria de Fátima Sanchez**, Colégio Salesiano Sta. Teresinha; **Regina C. B. Saponara**, Colégio N. S. do Sion; **Neuza C. Senna**, Colégio Henri Wallon; **Camila Toniolo Silva**, Colégio I. L. Peretz; **Izaura Valverde**, Nova Escola.

Curitiba Liana Andrade, Colégio Medianeira; **Bianca S. Borges**, Colégio Bom Jesus; **Rosana Fernandes**, Colégio Bom Jesus; **Cecilia Honorio**, Colégio Medianeira; **Regina Linzmayer**, Colégio Bom Jesus; **Maria Cecília Piccoli**, Colégio N. S. Sion; **Ana L. Z. Pinto**, Colégio Bom Jesus; **Mary C. M. dos Santos**, Colégio Bom Jesus; **Andrea S. M. Souza**, Colégio Bom Jesus; **Juçara M. S. Tadra**, Colégio Bom Jesus.

Rio de Janeiro Alcyrema R. Castro, Colégio N. S. da Assunção; **Renata Frazão**, Colégio Verbo Divino; **Claudia G. Goretti**, Colégio dos Jesuítas; **Letícia Leite**, Colégio Verbo Divino; **Livia Mercuri**, WSA Idiomas; **Marta Moraes**, Colégio São Vicente de Paulo; **Claudia C. Rosa**, Colégio Santa Mônica.

Belo Horizonte Júnia Barcelos, Colégio Santo Agostinho; **Rachel Farias**, Colégio Edna Roriz; **Renato Galil**, Colégio Santo Agostinho; **Katia R. P. A. Lima**, Colégio Santa Maria; **Gleides A. Nonato**, Colégio Arnaldo; **Luciana Queiros**, Instituto Itapoã; **Flávia Samarane**, Colégio Logosófico González Pecotche; **Adriana Zardini**, UFMG.

Brasília José Eugenio F. Alvim, CIL – 01; **Rosemberg Andrade**, Colégio Presbiteriano Mackenzie; **Euzenira Araújo**, CIL – Gama; **Michelle Câmara**, CIL – Gama; **Kátia Falcomer**, Casa Thomas Jefferson; **Almerinda B. Garibaldi**, CIL – Taguatinga; **Michelle Gheller**, CIL – Taguatinga; **Anabel Cervo Lima**, CIL – Brasília; **Ana Lúcia F. de Morais**, CIL – Brazilândia; **Antonio José O. Neto**, CIL – Ceilândia; **Maria da Graça Nóbile**, Colégio Presbiteriano Mackenzie; **Denise A. Nunes**, CIL – Gama; **Suzana Oliveira**, CIL – Taguatinga; **Andréa Pacheco**, Colégio Marista João Paulo II; **Simone Peixoto**, CIL – Brazilândia; **Érica S. Rodrigues**, Colégio Presbiteriano Mackenzie; **Isaura Rodrigues**, CIL – Ceilândia; **Camila Salmazo**, Colégio Marista João Paulo II; **Maria da Guia Santos**, CIL – Gama; **Dóris Scolmeister**, CIL – Gama; **Rejane M. C. de Souza**, Colégio Santa Rosa; **Isabel Teixeira**, CIL – Taguatinga; **Marina Vazquez**, CIL – Gama.

Questionnaires

Brazil Maria Heloísa Alves Audino, Colégio São Teodoro de Nossa Senhora de Sion; **Gleides A. Nonato**, Colégio Amaldo; **Gustavo Henrique Pires**, Instituto Presbiteriano de Educação; **Marta Gabriella Brunale dos Reis**, Colégio Integrado Jaó; **Paula Conti dos Reis Santos**, Colégio Anglo-Latino; **Tânia M. Sasaki**, High Five Language Center.

South Korea Don M. Ahn, EDLS; **Don Bryant**, OnGok Middle School.

Taiwan John A. Davey, Stella Matutina Girls' High School, Taichung City, Taiwan; **Gregory Alan Gwenossis**, Victoria Academy.

Japan Simon Butler, Fujimi Junior and Senior High School; **Yuko Hiroyama**, Pioneer Language School; **Mark Itoh**, Honjo East Senior High School Affiliated Junior High School; **Norio Kawakubo**, Yokohama YMCA ACT; **Michael Lambe**, Kyoto Girls Junior and Senior High School; **John George Lowery**, Dokkyo Junior High School/John G. Lowery School of English; **Jacques Stearn**, American Language School; **Simon Wykamp**, Hiroshima Johoku Junior and Senior High School.

Illustration Credits

Chuck Gonzales 11, 18, 37, 46, 60, 84, 88, 98, 120
Adam Hurwitz 105
Kim Johnson 10, 32, 56, 99, 112
Frank Montagna 6, 28, 51, 59, 72, 102
Rob Schuster 30, 115, 116, 120, 121
James Yamasaki 16, 17, 42, 43, 48, 64, 95, 114

Photo Acknowledgements

The authors and publishers acknowledge the following sources of copyright material and are grateful for the permissions granted. While every effort has been made, it has not always been possible to identify the sources of all the material used, or to trace all copyright holders. If any omissions are brought to our notice, we will be happy to include the appropriate acknowledgements on reprinting.

Student's Book

p. iv (Unit 1): ©Minerva Studio/Shutterstock; p. iv (Unit 2): ©Blutgruppe/Corbis; p. iv (Unit 3): ©OJO Images Ltd/Alamy; p. iv (Unit 5): ©FOX/Getty Images; p. iv (Unit 6): ©Nick Savage/Alamy; p. iv (Unit 7): ©Philip Lee Harvey/The Image Bank/Getty Images; p. iv (Unit 8): ©NASA/Space Frontiers/Getty Images; p. 5: ©Stuwdamdorp/Alamy; p. 7 (TL): ©Mark E. Gibson/CORBIS; p. 7 (TR): ©PhotoAlto sas/Alamy; p. 7 (BL): ©Lourens Smak/Alamy; p. 7 (BR): ©GoGo Images Corporation/Alamy; p. 8 (TL, TR): ©Harry How/Getty Images; p. 8 (BL): ©JEAN-CHRISTOPHE VERHAEGEN/AFP/Getty Images; p. 9: ©Design Pics Inc/Alamy; p. 12: ©EMMANUEL DUNAND/AFP/Getty Images; p. 13: ©Minerva Studio/Shutterstock; p. 14: ©MShieldsPhotos/Alamy; p. 15 (TL, TR): ©Gregg DeGuire/WireImage/Getty Images; p. 15 (BL): ©Barry King/FilmMagic/Getty Images; p. 15 (BR): ©Kevork Djansezian/Getty Images; p. 19: ©Sylvain Sonnet/The Image Bank/Getty Images; p. 20 (TL): ©Stephen Derr/The Image Bank/Getty Images; p. 20 (TC): ©Tetra Images/Getty Images; p. 20 (TR): ©Maria Teijeiro/

Photodisc/Getty Images; p. 20 (BL): ©rolfo/Moment/Getty Images; p. 20 (BC): ©John Henley/Blend Images/Getty Images; p. 20 (BR): ©Nisian Hughes/Photodisc/Getty Images; p. 21 (TL): ©Chris Ryan/OJO Images/Getty Images; p. 21 (TR): ©Keith Leighton/Alamy; p. 21 (CR): ©-M-IS-H-A-/iStock/Getty Images Plus/Getty Images; p. 21 (BL): ©Tom Strattman/Getty Images; p. 21 (BR): ©Fuse/Getty Images; p. 22 (TL): replace with: ©dmac/Alamy; p. 22 (TC): ©Colin Utz Photography/Alamy; p. 22 (TR): ©Hemera Technologies/AbleStock.com/Getty Images Plus/Getty Images; p. 22 (CL): ©Greg Balfour Evans/Alamy; p. 22 (C): ©Image Source/Digital Vision/Getty Images; p. 22 (CR): ©monkeybusinessimages/Stock/Getty Images Plus/Getty Images; p. 22 (BL): ©Jupiterimages/Photolibrary/Getty Images; p. 22 (BC): ©Images-USA/Alamy; p. 22 (BR): ©Silvia Morara/Corbis; p. 23: ©Image Source/Getty Images; p. 24 (L): ©Sean Justice/The Image Bank/Getty Images; p. 24 (C): ©Nord, 62_/Getty Images; p. 24 (R): ©Monkey Business Images/Shutterstock; p. 26 (T): ©Aerial Archives/Alamy; p. 26 (B): ©Blutgruppe/Corbis; p. 27: ©Javier Pierini/Taxi/Getty Images; p. 31 (T): ©145/Scott Quinn Photography/Ocean/Corbis; p. 31 (B): ©elenaleonova/iStock/Getty Images Plus/Getty Images; p. 32: ©Westend61/Getty Images; p. 38 (T): ©John Elk III/Lonely Planet Images/Getty Images; p. 38 (B): ©Donald Miralle/Getty Images; p. 39 (L): ©Vibrant Image Studio/Shutterstock; p. 39 (CL): ©DigitalVues/Alamy; p. 39 (CR): ©monticello/iStock/Getty Images Plus/Getty Images; p. 39 (R): ©efreet/iStock/Getty Images Plus/Getty Images; p. 40 (T): ©Jenny Acheson/Iconica/GettyImages; p. 40 (B): ©OJO Images Ltd/Alamy; p. 41: ©Rubberball/Mike Kemp/Getty Images; p. 45: ©Andersen Ross/Stockbyte/Getty Images; p. 47: ©Tyler Edwards/Digital Vision/Getty Images; p. 49: ©Karen Moskowitz/The Image Bank/Getty Images; p. 50 (TL): ©Andrea Lynn/Photolibrary/Getty Images; p. 50 (TR): ©Arctic-Images/The Image Bank/Getty Images; p. 50 (CL): ©Bilgin Sasmaz/Anadolu Agency/Getty Images; p. 50 (CR): ©Nik Taylor/Alamy; p. 50 (BL): ©Adrian Peacock/Photodisc/Getty Images; p. 50 (BR): ©Paul Barton/Corbis; p. 54: ©Gary John Norman/Photodisc/Getty Images; p. 55: ©Anthony Hatley/Alamy; p. 57: ©Paul Gilham/Getty Images; p. 60 (L): ©Franziska Krug/Getty Images; p. 60 (C): ©Jon Kopaloff/FilmMagic/Getty Images; p. 60 (R): ©Karwai Tang/WireImage/Getty Images; p. 61 (T): ©Franziska Krug/Getty Images; p. 61 (C): ©Jason Kempin/CDG/Getty Images; p. 61 (B): ©Dave M. Benett/Getty Images; p. 62: ©Kevin Winter/WireImage/Getty Images; p. 63: ©George Doyle/Stockbyte/Getty Images; p. 65: ©Gene Lower/Getty Images; p. 66 (TL): ©Vince Bucci/Getty Images; p. 66 (TC): ©Mike Marsland/WireImage/Getty Images; p. 66 (TR): ©Most Wanted/REX Shutterstock; p. 66 (BL): ©Kuttig - Travel/Alamy; p. 66 (BC): ©Hiroko Masuike/Getty Images; p. 66 (BR): ©Gunnar Pippel/Shutterstock; p. 67 (Jamie Foxx): ©GABRIEL BOUYS/AFP/Getty Images; p. 67 (guitar): ©Olga Miltsova/Shutterstock; p. 67 (Paramount): ©CHARLES SYKES/REX Shutterstock; p. 67 (statue): ©Scott Olson/Getty Images; p. 67 (TV): ©GeorgeMPhotography/Shutterstock; p. 68: ©FOX/Getty Images; p. 69: ©Kevin Wheal/Alamy; p. 71 (L): ©Rob Lewine/Getty Images; p. 71 (R): ©Ryan McVay/Photodisc/Getty Images; p. 74 (L): ©Dafinka/Shutterstock; p. 74 (C): ©Fuse/Getty Images; p. 74 (R): ©Nick Savage/Alamy; p. 75 (L): ©Tony Anderson/The Image Bank/Getty Images; p. 75 (R): ©karamysh/Shutterstock; p. 76: ©Image Source/Getty Images; p. 78 (L): ©Jeff Gross/Getty Images; p. 78 (R): ©ZUMA/REX Shutterstock; p. 79: ©Jared Wickerham/Getty Images; p. 80: ©Doug Waters/Photodisc/Getty Images; p. 81 (T): ©Lester Cohen/WireImage/Getty Images; p. 81 (CL): ©Jo Hale/Getty Images; p. 81 (CR): ©Vince Bucci/Getty Images; p. 81 (B): ©John Shearer/WireImage/Getty Images; p. 82 (T): ©Everett/REX Shutterstock; p. 82 (B): ©Matt Campbell//AFP/Getty Images; p. 83: ©Mark A Johnson/Photodisc/Getty Image; p. 86 (L): ©John Eder/The Image Bank/Getty Images; p. 86 (R): ©Radius Images/Getty Images Plus/Getty Images; p. 87: ©Philip Lee Harvey/The Image Bank/Getty Images; p. 89: ©TEMPLE HILL ENTERTAINMENT/THE KOBAL COLLECTION; p. 90 (T): ©Nitr/Shutterstock; p. 90 (B): ©Nata-Lia/Shutterstock; p. 92 (L): ©Dream-Pictures/The Image Bank/Getty Images; p. 92 (R): ©Imeh Akpanudosen/Getty Images; p. 93: ©Mat Hayward/Getty Images; p. 95 (T): ©Tom-Kli/Shutterstock; p. 95 (B): ©Steve Buckley/Shutterstock; p. 96 (L): ©leungchopan/Shutterstock; p. 96 (R): ©Image Source/Alamy; p. 97: ©Dan Breckwoldt/Shutterstock; p. 99 (L): ©ene/Shutterstock; p. 99 (R): ©GeorgeMPhotography/Shutterstock; p. 100 (TL): ©Roman Sigaev/Shutterstock; p. 100 (TC): ©HotNYCNews/Alamy; p. 100 (TR): ©Andrea Izzotti/Shutterstock; p. 100 (BL): ©Nicolas Russell/The Image Bank/Getty Images; p. 100 (BC): ©Noah Graham/NBAE/Getty Images; p. 100 (BR): ©WLDavies/iStock/Getty Images Plus/Getty Images; p. 101: ©LOOK Die Bildagentur der Fotografen GmbH/Alamy; p. 104 (T): ©AfriPics.com/Alamy; p. 104 (C): ©David Edwards/National Geographic Creative/Corbis; p. 104 (B): ©FADEL SENNA/AFP/Getty Images; p. 106 (TL): ©Digital Vision/Photodisc/Getty Images; p. 106 (TC): ©bokan/Shutterstock; p. 106 (TR): ©NASA/Space Frontiers/Getty Images; p. 106 (CL): ©Tetra Images/Getty Images; p. 106 (C): ©EITAN ABRAMOVICH/AFP/Getty Images; p. 106 (CR): ©ERproductions Ltd/Blend Images/Getty Images; p. 106 (BL): ©Eric Farrelly/Alamy; p. 106 (BC): ©Dean Golja/Digital Vision/Getty Images; p. 106 (BR): ©Indiascapes/Alamy; p. 107 (L): ©Design Pics/Colleen Cahill/Getty Images; p. 107 (R): ©Zen Sekizawa/Taxi/Getty Images; p. 107 (CL): ©Paul Simcock/Photodisc/Getty Images; p. 107 (CR): ©Nadezhda V. Kulagina/Shutterstock; p. 109 (L): ©Strahil Dimitrov/Shutterstock; p. 109 (C): ©Digital Vision/Getty Images; p. 109 (R): ©Andersen Ross/Digital Vision/Getty Images; p. 110 (T): ©Brian Ach/The Lasker Foundation/Getty Images; p. 110 (C): ©Jason Merritt/Getty Images; p. 110 (B): ©Alberto E. Rodriguez/Getty Images; p. 111: ©Neamov/Shutterstock; p. 117 (L): ©Yellowdog Productions/Digital Vision/Getty Images; p. 117 (TCL): ©Jupiterimages/Pixland/Getty Images Plus/Getty Images; p. 117 (TC): ©Hero Images/Getty Images; p. 117 (TCR): ©Westend61/Getty Images; p. 117 (R): ©Kaz Chiba/Photodisc/Getty Images; p. 117 (BCL): ©ColorBlind Images/Iconica/Getty Images; p. 117 (BC): ©Jack Hollingsworth/Photodisc/Getty Images; p. 117 (BCR): ©LWA/Dann Tardif/Blend Images/Getty Images; p. 118: ©pixelheadphoto/Shutterstock; p. 125: ©Chirag Wakaskar/WireImage/Getty Images; p. 126: ©Mark Bowden/iStock/Getty Images Plus/Getty Images; p. 127: ©Kali Nine LLC/iStock/Getty Images Plus/Getty Images; p. 128: ©Steffen Schnur/Moment Open/Getty Images; p. 129: ©Jon Feingersh/Blend Images/Getty Images; p. 130 (L): ©F. A. Alba/Shutterstock; p. 130 (TR): ©Kaz Chiba/Digital Vision/Getty Images; p. 130 (BC): ©Juanmonino/iStock/Getty Images Plus/Getty Images; p. 130 (BR): ©Bet_Noire/iStock/Getty Images Plus/Getty Images; p. 131: ©Pixland/Getty Images Plus/Getty Images; p. 132 (T): ©Elnur/Shutterstock; p. 132 (C): ©niwat chaiyawoot/Shutterstock; p. 132 (B): ©Olga Miltsova/Shutterstock; p. 133: ©Jim West/Alamy.

Commissioned photography by Lawrence Migdale for pages 2, 3, 4, 25, 36, 52, 58, 64, 73, 94, 103, 108.

Cover photograph by ©Siberia - Video and Photo/Shutterstock

Art Direction, book design, and layout services: A+ Comunicação, São Paulo

Notes